D1038813

THE BOOK OF
OUR HERITAGE

Eliyahu Kitov

THE BOOK OF OUR HERITAGE

The Jewish year and its days of significance

SPECIAL EDITION

The Month of Adar

Translated from the Hebrew SEFER HA-TODA'AH
by NATHAN BULMAN

Revised by Dovid Landesman

FELDHEIM PUBLISHERS

Jerusalem / New York

ISBN — 0-87306-159-4

Copyright © 1995/5755 by Yad Eliyahu Kitov

All rights reserved.
No part of this publication may be translated,
reproduced, stored in a retrieval system or transmitted,
in any form or by any means, electronic, photocopying,
recording or otherwise, without prior permission in
writing from the copyright holder and publisher.

FELDHEIM PUBLISHERS
POB 35002 / Jerusalem, Israel

200 Airport Executive Park
Nanuet, N.Y. 10954

Printed and bound in U.S.A. by
Noble Book Press Corp.
New York, NY 10001

CONTENTS

✍ This symbol indicates a halachah — a Torah precept or
Rabbinic law.
✿ This symbol precedes a *minhag* — a custom observed in many
households or in various Jewish communities.

Adar

CHAPTER ONE

ADAR

The month of Adar is the last month of the Hebrew year, based on the count that begins with Nisan, and is referred to as such in Scripture (*Divrei ha-Yamim* I 27:15, *Esther* 9:1). In a leap year, when a second month of Adar is added to the calendar, it too is referred to as the twelfth month. Thus, we see that the verse states: AND IN THE TWELFTH MONTH, IN THE MONTH OF ADAR (*Esther* 9:1). According to tradition, Haman's plot to kill the Jews took place in a leap year and the miraculous deliverance took place in the second Adar which the verse refers to as the twelfth month.

Rosh Chodesh Adar always consists of two days. In a leap year, the second Adar also has a two day *Rosh Chodesh* — the first day being counted as the thirtieth day of the first Adar. Adar always consists of twenty-nine days; thus *Rosh Chodesh* Nisan is always one day.

WHEN ADAR BEGINS, JOY IS INCREASED

Our Sages taught: Just as when Av begins our joy is reduced, so too when Adar begins our joy is increased. R. Pappa said: Therefore a Jew who is involved in litigation with a non-Jew should avoid him during Av, for it is a time of ill omen for him. And he should attempt to meet him in court in Adar, for it is a time of good omen for him (*Ta'anis* 29a). Heaven directs merit toward a period worthy of merit, and joy towards a month marked by joy. There is no month that is more joyous than Adar, for during Adar there is great bounty which is hidden and the evil eyes of Israel's enemies cannot affect this bounty.

When the wicked Haman astrologically sought to establish the
month during which Israel would be most vulnerable, he cast
lots in order to determine when he should bring his evil plans
to fruition. The lot fell on the month of Adar, but Haman was
unaware that it was in this month that the Jews were at their
strongest. Thus, when the month that he planned to turn into
grief and mourning was transformed into a month of rejoicing
and celebration, the happiness of the Jews was that much greater. The month of Adar became a symbol of joy for them.

THE SEVENTH OF ADAR

The seventh of Adar is the day on which Moshe *Rabbenu* was
born, and the day on which he passed away one hundred and
twenty years later. God completes the years of the righteous to
the day and month, as the verse (*Shemos* 23:26) states: I SHALL COM-
PLETE THE NUMBER OF YOUR DAYS.

It is customary among the *chassidim* and pious to fast on the
seventh of Adar, and to recite the special *tikun* prayer for the
day which is found in the *siddur*. The death of the righteous is a
source of atonement, as are fasting, prayers and repentance.
When all of these sources of atonement are combined, Israel
achieves total forgiveness.

WAITING FOR SALVATION

On the seventh of Adar, every man should pay heed to two
concerns and should resolve to become constantly aware of
them; to wait for salvation and to fear Divine judgement.

What is meant by the phrase "waiting for salvation"? A lesson
that sheds light on this can be drawn from the birth of Moshe
Rabbenu. The circumstances that surrounded Moshe's birth
were sad. Pharaoh had decreed: Every son that is born shall be

cast by you into the river. For three and a third years, Pharaoh's officers and people had lurked in ambush for every pregnant Jewish woman. When the time to give birth came and a son was born, they would seize the infant and cast him into the river. Every Jewish child emerged from his mother's womb marked for death. All of Israel lived in anguish and despair. When Amram — leader of the generation — saw his people suffering so greatly, he cried out: "Our efforts are for naught." He thereupon divorced his wife so that they would not bring additional children into the world. At this time, his wife Yocheved was already three months pregnant with Moshe.

When the nation of Israel saw what Amram had done, they too divorced their wives. But at that very hour, the Divine spirit rested upon Miriam, who was but five years old, and she said: "My mother is destined to bear a son who will redeem Israel." Her words infused her father and mother with renewed courage and faith, and they remarried. All of Israel followed their example and soon, the one who would redeem Israel was born.

How great was the anxiety and anguish when Moshe was born, for Pharaoh's entire nation — men, women and children — sought to find him and kill him. And behold, after he was born, he too was cast defenseless into the river.

And even when he was saved, he still faced great danger. While still a nursing infant he was cast into the den of the lions, for he was raised in the house of Pharaoh — a house from which relentless anger and destruction emerged against Israel. Moshe was but an infant — he knew not his father nor recognized his mother nor had he even ever seen his people. The wicked could raise him to become an enemy of Israel — to join with them in tormenting Israel. Indeed, Amram's cry of anguish seemed to be justified. "Our efforts are for naught."

Come and see how great is the faith of those who look forward to salvation! Had it not been for the faith that pulsed in Miriam's heart and in the heart of others who shared her conviction, had Moshe not been born, what purpose would there be for the world which would have reverted to formlessness and emptiness? Now that Moshe was born — and even though he was placed within the lion's den — he was destined to emerge to save his people and bring enlightenment to the entire world for all generations. Even the wicked would be forced to admit, God is righteous.

FEARING DIVINE JUDGEMENT

Moshe *Rabbenu* was the master of all of the prophets. From the day of his birth the spirit of prophecy rested upon him. He brought Israel salvation and performed wondrous miracles in Egypt on their behalf. He split the sea and paved a road to heaven for them. He battled with the angels and received the Torah of fire. He sat at the foot of the Heavenly throne and spoke to God directly. He taught Torah to all of Israel and provided their sustenance during their forty year sojourn in the desert. He waged war against the mighty kings, Sichon and Og, and caused the sun and the moon to stand in their places.

Yet, when he committed a minor sin in the incident of the waters of Merivah and the sanctity of God's name was diminished as a result, his death was decreed and he was denied entry into the Land of Israel. Neither his own great merit, nor all of his achievements on behalf of Israel could protect him from the Divine attribute of justice — the attribute which is the truth of the Creator.

How awesome is the depth of Divine judgement and how fearful must man be of inadvertent sin!

EXCERPTS FROM THE *MIDRASHIM* ON THE BIRTH OF MOSHE

AND A MAN WENT FROM THE HOUSE OF LEVI (*Shemos* 2:1) — where did he go? R. Yehudah bar Ravina said: He "went" according to his daughter's advice. We learned: Amram was the leader of his generation. When he saw that the wicked Pharaoh had decreed, "Every son that is born, you shall cast him into the river," he said, "Our efforts are for naught." He thereupon decided to divorce his wife and all of them [i.e., the children of Israel] also decided to divorce their wives. His daughter then said to him, "Father, your decree is harsher than that of Pharaoh, for Pharaoh's decree only applied to the males, whereas your decree applies to both males and females. Moreover, Pharaoh's decree is only relevant in this world whereas your decree is relevant both in this world and in the World to Come. Because Pharaoh is wicked, it is doubtful whether his decree will endure. But you are righteous and your decree will surely endure." Amram thereupon remarried his wife and the rest of them also remarried their wives (*Sotah* 12a).

AND HE TOOK A DAUGHTER OF LEVI (*Shemos* 2:1) — The verse does not state, "and he remarried," but rather, "he took." R. Yehudah bar Zevina explained: He treated her as if she was a new bride. He set her in a palace with Miriam and Aharon dancing before her. The celestial angels then said, THE MOTHER OF THE SONS REJOICES (*Shemos Rabbah* 1).

AND THE WOMAN CONCEIVED AND BORE A SON (ibid. 2:2) — Was she not already three months pregnant? R. Yehudah bar Zevina explained: Her delivery is compared to the time of conception. Just as the conception was without pain, so was the delivery without pain (*Sotah* 12a).

AND SHE SAW THAT HE WAS GOOD (ibid.) — R. Meir said: His name was *tov* [good]. R. Yehudah said: He was worthy of prophecy. Others explained: He was born already circumcised. The

13

Sages said: When Moshe was born the entire world was filled with light. The verse here states: AND SHE SAW THAT HE WAS GOOD and elsewhere the verse (*Bereshis* 1:4) states: AND GOD SAW THE LIGHT THAT IT WAS GOOD (*Yalkut Shimoni* 166).

Why did she [Yocheved, Moshe's mother] cast him into the river? She wanted the astrologers to think that he had already been thrown into the water so that they would not continue to search for him.

When Moshe was cast into the water, they [the Egyptians] said: "Their redeemer has been cast into the water," and the decree [that every Jewish male be thrown into the Nile] was immediately suspended.

R. Acha bar Chanina said: That day was the sixth of Sivan. The celestial angels said to God, "Master of the Universe, shall the one who is destined to receive the Torah on Mt. Sinai on this date be struck by the water on this date!"

SHALL I GO AND CALL YOU A WET-NURSE FROM AMONG THE HEBREWS (*Shemos* 2:7) — Why did Miriam specify from among the Hebrews? Was Moshe prohibited from nursing from the breast of a gentile woman?... She [Pharaoh's daughter] had brought Moshe to be nursed by all the Egyptian women, but he had refused. And why did he refuse? God said: "Shall the mouth which is destined to speak with Me nurse from an impure source?!"

Alternatively, why did he refuse to nurse from them? God said: "This person is destined to speak with Me. Tomorrow the Egyptian women will brag and declare, 'This one who speaks with the *Shechinah* — I nursed him!'" (*Shemos Rabbah* 1).

EXCERPTS FROM THE *MIDRASHIM* REGARDING MOSHE'S DEATH

AND GOD SAID TO MOSHE, YOUR DAYS HAVE DRAWN NEAR TO DIE (*Devarim* 31:14) — The Sages explained: It is difficult for God to decree that the righteous shall die, as the verse (*Tehillim* 116:15) states: THE DEATH OF HIS PIOUS ONES IS PRECIOUS IN THE EYES OF GOD. Proof for this can be drawn from our verse. Moshe should have been told, "Behold, you shall die." But God did not say this; rather, instead of mentioning Moshe, He referred to his *days* as drawing near to death.

AND GOD SAID TO MOSHE, YOUR DAYS HAVE DRAWN NEAR TO DIE — this explains the verses (*Iyov* 20:6-7) which state: IF HIS HEIGHTS SHALL RISE TO THE HEAVENS AND HIS HEAD SHALL REACH THE CLOUDS...HE WILL PERISH. THOSE WHO SEE WILL ASK, WHERE IS HE? Regarding what was this verse said? Regarding the day of death, for even if a man were to sprout wings like a bird and ascend to heaven, when the time of his death comes, his wings break and he falls. IF HIS HEIGHTS SHALL RISE TO THE HEAVENS — regarding whom was this said? Regarding Moshe, for he ascended to the firmament, and his feet stepped on the mist, and he was like one of the angels, and he spoke to God directly and received the Torah from His hand. Yet, when his time came, God said to him: "Your days have drawn near to die."

When Moshe saw that the Divine decree had been sealed, he drew a small circle and said: "Master of the Universe, I will not move from here until You revoke the decree." He then put on

15

sackcloth and ashes and stood in supplication and prayer before God until the heavens and earth and nature itself began to tremble. They said: "Perhaps the will of God is to renew His world!" A heavenly voice replied: "It is not yet God's will to renew His world. Rather, in His hand the soul of every living being rests."

What did God do at this time? He proclaimed at each gate of each firmament that Moshe's prayer not be accepted and not be brought before Him, for the decree against him had been sealed. When the sounds of his prayer rose upwards in ever increasing strength, God called the celestial angels and said to them: "Quickly descend and close the gates of every firmament," for Moshe's prayer was like a sharp sword which pierces and slices away every obstacle.

Moshe then said to God: "Master of the Universe, the effort I made and the pain I endured so that Israel would have faith in Your name, are clear and known to You. How much anguish I suffered on their behalf until I inculcated them with the Torah and mitzvos! I said to myself: 'Just as I saw their pain, so too will I witness the good that will be theirs.' Now that the good has arrived, You say to me, YOU SHALL NOT CROSS THIS JORDAN RIVER (Devarim 3:27). You are making Your Torah untruthful, for the verse states: ON HIS DAY [THE DAY THAT HE WORKS] YOU SHALL PAY HIS WAGES (ibid. 24:15). Is this the recompense for the forty years of labor that I worked until I made them into a holy and faithful nation?" God answered him: "It is a decree before Me!"

Moshe thereupon responded and said: "Master of the Universe, if I cannot enter [the Land of Israel] alive, allow me to enter dead, just as the bones of Yosef were allowed to enter." God answered: "Moshe, when Yosef came to Egypt, he did not pretend to be a gentile, but you — when you came to Midian — pretended to be a gentile [for Yisro's daughters told their father regarding Moshe, 'An Egyptian man saved us,' and Moshe knew that they said this and remained silent]."

Moshe then said: "Master of the Universe, if You will not allow me to enter the Land of Israel, let me remain like the animals of the fields who eat grass, drink water and see the world — let my soul be like one of them!" God answered him: IT IS TOO MUCH FOR YOU (ibid. 3:26).

Moshe then said: "Master of the Universe, if this is impossible, then let me stay in this world like a bird who flies in all four directions, gathers its food daily and at night returns to its nest — let my soul be like one of them!" God answered him: "It is too much for you."

When Moshe saw that his pleas were not accepted, he went to heaven and earth and pleaded: "Seek mercy for me!" They responded: "Rather than seeking mercy for you, we should seek mercy for ourselves, for the verse (Yeshayahu 51:6) states: FOR THE HEAVENS SHALL DISSIPATE LIKE SMOKE AND THE EARTH WILL ERODE LIKE A GARMENT."

He then went to the sun and the moon and pleaded: "Seek mercy for me!" They responded: "Rather than seeking mercy for you, we should seek mercy for ourselves, for the verse (ibid. 24:23) states: AND THE MOON SHALL BE EMBARRASSED AND THE SUN ASHAMED."

He then went to the stars and the constellations and pleaded: "Seek mercy for me!" They responded: "Rather than seeking mercy for you, we should seek mercy for ourselves, for the verse (ibid. 34:4) states: AND THE HOSTS OF HEAVENS SHALL BE ERASED."

He then went to the mountains and the valleys and pleaded: "Seek mercy for me!" They responded: "Rather than seeking mercy for you, we should seek mercy for ourselves, for the verse (ibid. 54:10) states: FOR THE MOUNTAINS SHALL BE UPROOTED AND THE VALLEYS UNSETTLED."

He then went to the sea and pleaded: "Seek mercy for me!" The sea responded: "Son of Amram! Why is today different than other days? Are you not the son of Amram who approached me with your staff, striking me and splitting me into twelve paths and I could not resist you because of the *Shechinah* which strode by your right side! And now, what has come upon you?"

When the sea reminded him of what he had done when he was younger, Moshe cried out: WHO WILL MAKE ME LIKE [I WAS] IN THE MONTHS THAT PASSED (*Iyov* 29:2)? When I stood before you [i.e., the sea], I was the ruler of the world, and now I prostrate myself and no one pays me any attention!"

Moshe then went to the angel of the inner chamber and said: "Seek mercy for me, that I might not die!" He replied: "Moshe, my master, for what purpose is this effort? I have heard from behind the curtain that your prayers in this matter shall not be heard."

Moshe then placed his hands on his head and cried out: "To whom shall I go that they might plead for mercy?" At that moment, God was angry with him, until he said this verse: GOD, GOD, THE LORD WHO IS MERCIFUL AND GRACIOUS (*Shemos* 34:6).

The [anger of the] spirit of Holiness subsided, and God said to Moshe: "Moshe, I have taken two oaths. One, that I would destroy Israel for what they had done then [i.e., the golden calf], and one that you are to die and not enter the Land of Israel. The oath which I took regarding Israel I annulled because of you, for you said, FORGIVE THEM I PLEAD (*Bemidbar* 14:19). And now, once again you ask that I nullify My desire and fulfill yours, for you say, LET ME CROSS [INTO THE LAND OF ISRAEL], I PLEAD (*Devarim* 3:25). You are trying to hold the rope from both ends. If you ask that I fulfill your request of LET ME CROSS, then withdraw your request of FORGIVE THEM. And if you wish Me to fulfill your request of FORGIVE THEM, then withdraw your request of LET ME CROSS!"

When Moshe heard this, he said: "Master of the Universe, let Moshe and a thousand like him perish, but let not a single fingernail of Israel be injured!"

Moshe said to God: "Master of the Universe, the feet which ascended to the firmament, the face which greeted the *Shechinah* and the hands which received the Torah from Your hand — shall they lick the dust?" God answered: "Such is the thought which has come before Me and this is the way of the world — each generation has its teachers, each generation has those who sustain it and each generation has its leaders. Until now, it was your role to serve before Me. Now, the time has come for your disciple Yehoshua to serve."

Moshe then said: "If I am to die because of Yehoshua, I shall go and become his disciple." God responded: "If you wish to do so, go and do it."

Moshe rose and entered Yehoshua's doorway. Yehoshua was teaching, and Moshe stood and bent down with his hand covering his heart. Yehoshua was made unable to notice him so that Moshe might grieve and accept death.

All of Israel went to Moshe's doorway to learn Torah, and asked: "Where has Moshe gone?" They were told: "He went to Yehoshua's doorway." They went and found him at the entrance, and Yehoshua was seated while Moshe was standing. They said to Yehoshua: "What has come over you, that Moshe stands while you sit!" When Yehoshua looked up and saw him, he immediately tore his clothes and cried out: "My master, my master, my father, my father!"

Israel then said to Moshe: "Moshe, our master, teach us Torah!" He replied: "I do not have permission." They said to him: "We will not leave you." A Divine voice called out: "Learn from Yehoshua!" They thereupon accepted it upon themselves to sit and study with Yehoshua.

Yehoshua seated himself at the head with Moshe on his right and the sons of Aharon on his left. He then taught and expounded in Moshe's presence. At this time, the chain of wisdom was taken and passed to Yehoshua.

When they went out to walk, Moshe strode on Yehoshua's left. They entered the Tent of Meeting and the pillar of clouds descended and separated them. When the pillar of clouds ascended, Moshe asked: "What did the Divine word say to you?"

Yehoshua answered: "When the Divine word was revealed to you, did I know what was said?"

At this point, Moshe cried out and said: "May I die a hundred deaths but be spared jealousy! Master of the Worlds, until now I asked for life. Now, my soul is given to You."

R. Yoshiah said: At this time, Moshe accorded Yehoshua great honor and respect in Israel's presence, and a proclamation went forth throughout the encampment of Israel that stated: "Come and hear the words of the new prophet who will rise for us on this day."

All of Israel went to pay honor to Yehoshua. Moshe then ordered that a golden throne be brought, as well as a crown of gems, royal headwear and a purple robe. Moshe stood and arranged the chairs of the *Sanhedrin*, of the heads of the regiments and the *kohanim*. He then approached Yehoshua, dressed him, placed the crown on his head, sat him on the golden throne and appointed an interpreter to explain his teachings to all of Israel and to Moshe, his master.

Moshe said to Yehoshua: "Come and I will kiss you." Yehoshua came and Moshe kissed him, and while weeping on his shoulder, he blessed him again and said: "May you live in peace and may Israel, my nation, live in peace. They never were satisfied with me for as long as I served, because of the warnings and admonitions which I addressed to them."

Moshe then began to bless each tribe separately. When he saw that the time of his death was drawing near, he included them all in one blessing. He said to them: "I have caused you much anguish with the Torah and mitzvos [which I taught you]. Forgive me!"

They answered: "Our teacher, our master! We also have caused you to become angry and have caused you great hardship. Forgive us!"

He answered: "It is forgiven."

A heavenly voice then said: "Moshe, why do you cause yourself anguish? Your life in this world is but another half an hour."

When Moshe saw the measure of the world and the great salvation and consolation that God was destined to bring Israel, he said to them: FORTUNATE ARE YOU, ISRAEL, WHO IS LIKE YOU, A PEOPLE WHOSE SALVATION IS IN GOD (Devarim 33:29). He then bid them peace, raised his voice and cried and said: "I shall see you in peace at the time of the resurrection of the dead."

He then left them weeping, and Israel too cried out bitterly. Moshe arose and rent his garment, took off his robe and covered his head like a mourner. He entered his tent and cried and said: "Woe is to my feet which did not step into the Land of Israel, woe is to my hands which did not pick its fruits, woe is to my palate which did not taste the produce of the land that flows with milk and honey!"

When Moshe had finished preparing his soul to face death, God said: WHO SHALL STAND FOR ME AGAINST THOSE WHO DO EVIL? (Tehillim 94:16). Who will stand up for Israel at the time of My anger? And who will stand up for them when my sons are en-

21

gaged in battle? And who shall seek mercy for them at the time when they sin before me?"

At this time, Metatron came and prostrated himself before God and said: "Master of the Universe, when Moshe was alive, he was Yours. And in his death, he is Yours."

God answered: "I will tell you a parable to which this is comparable. There was a king who had a son who incensed his father every day. His father wanted to kill him, but his mother saved him. When the mother died, the king began to weep. His servants said to him: 'Our master, the king, why do you weep?' He replied, 'I am not crying solely for my wife, but for her and for my son. Many times I became angry with him and sought to kill him, but his mother would save him from my hand.'"

This is what the Holy One, blessed is He, said to Metatron. "I do not weep for Moshe alone, but for him and for Israel. A number of times they angered Me and I became angry with them, but he stood in the breach so as to turn back My anger."

At this time, the Holy One, blessed is He, said to Gavriel: "Go and bring the soul of Moshe."

He said before Him: "Master of the Universe, he who is equal to six hundred thousand, how can I see his death?"

God said to Michoel: "Go and bring the soul of Moshe."

He said before Him: "I was his teacher and he was my disciple. How can I see his death?"

God said to Samael: "Go and bring the soul of Moshe."

The angel Samael, chief of the Satans, had been awaiting the soul of Moshe, saying: "When will the moment come when Moshe shall die and I shall descend and take his soul from him? When will the time come when Michoel will cry and my mouth will be filled with laughter?"

He clothed himself in anger, girded his sword, wrapped himself in cruelty and approached Moshe. He found him seated, writing the ineffable Divine name in a scroll, and the radiance of his appearance was like the radiance of the sun and he was like an angel of God.

He [Samael] immediately became frightened and began to tremble and could not find a way to begin to speak until Moshe said to him: "Wicked one, why are you here?" He replied: "I have come to take your soul."

He said to him: "Who sent you?"

He replied: "He who created every creature."

He [Moshe] said to him: "Go away from here, for I wish to praise God. I SHALL NOT DIE, BUT I SHALL LIVE AND TELL OF THE DEEDS OF GOD" (*Tehillim* 118:17).

He said to him: "Moshe, why are you haughty? He has those who can praise him — THE HEAVENS RECOUNT THE GLORY OF GOD" (ibid. 19:2).

Moshe answered him: "I shall silence them and praise Him — LISTEN, O HEAVENS AND I SHALL SPEAK, AND LET THE EARTH HEAR THE WORDS OF MY MOUTH" (*Devarim* 32:1).

He replied: "All the souls of those who come into the world are given in to my hands."

Moshe answered him: "I have greater power than anyone who has come into the world."

He asked him: "What is your power?"

Moshe answered him: "I am the son of Amram and I prophesied at the age of three and said, 'I am destined to receive the Torah from amidst the fire.' I entered the palace of the king and removed the crown from his [Pharaoh's] head. When I was eighty, I performed wonders and miracles in Egypt and I brought six hundred thousand people out before the eyes of the Egyptians. I split the sea into twelve channels. I ascended and paved a path in the heavens. I waged war with the angels and I vanquished the Heavenly hosts and revealed their secrets to mortal man. I spoke to the Holy One, blessed is He, face to face and received the Torah of fire from His right hand and taught it to Israel. I waged war with Sichon and Og, the two mightiest of the nations of the world, and I struck them with my staff and killed them. I caused the sun and the moon to stop at the height of their cycles — is there another among those who come into this world that can do these things? Go and flee; I will not give you my soul."

Samael immediately returned and reported what had happened before the Most High. The Holy One, blessed is He, said to him: "Go out and bring Moshe's soul." Samael unsheathed his sword and stood over Moshe. Moshe became angry with him and took his staff of God in his hand, which had the ineffable name of God engraved on it, and struck Samael with all his might until Samael fled. Moshe pursued him with the ineffable Name, and blinded him.

A Divine voice then came forth and said: "The time of your death has come." He replied: "Blessed is His name, who lives and endures forever." Moshe then said to Israel: "I ask of you, when you come to the Land of Israel, remember me and my corpse and say, 'Woe to the son of Amram, who ran before us like a steed and his corpse fell in the wilderness.'"

A Divine voice then came forth and said: "Within half a minute you are to depart from this world." He lifted his two arms and placed them on his heart, and said to Israel: "See the end of one who is flesh and blood."

At that time, Moshe stood and sanctified himself like the *serafim*. The Holy One, blessed is He, descended from the highest heaven to take Moshe's soul, and three ministering angels accompanied Him — Michoel, Gavriel and Zagzael. Michoel spread Moshe's bed, Gavriel spread a linen cloth under his head, and Zagzael placed one under his feet. Michoel stood at one side and Gavriel stood at the other.

God said to Moshe: "Moshe, close your eyes," and he closed his eyes. "Place your hands on your chest," and he placed his hands on his chest. "Bring your feet together," and he brought his feet together.

At that time, God called Moshe's soul and said to her: "My daughter, I assigned you one hundred and twenty years in Moshe's body. Now the time has come for you to depart. Emerge and do not delay."

She [Moshe's soul] responded: "Master of the Universe, I know that You are the Master of all spirits and the Master of all souls. You created me and You placed me in Moshe's body for one hundred and twenty years. And now, is there a more pure body in this world than that of Moshe? I love him and I do not wish to depart from him!"

God answered: "Emerge and I shall take you to the highest of heavens and seat you beneath the throne of My glory, near the cherubs and *serafim*." At that time, God kissed Moshe and took his soul with a kiss.

The spirit of Holiness wept and said: AND NO PROPHET LIKE MOSHE ROSE AGAIN IN ISRAEL (*Devarim* 34:10).

The heavens wept and said: THE PIOUS MAN HAS BEEN LOST FROM THE WORLD (*Michah* 7:2).

The earth wept and said: AND THERE IS NO RIGHTEOUSNESS AMONG MEN (ibid.).

The ministering angels wept and said: THE RIGHTEOUSNESS OF GOD HE DID (*Devarim* 33:21).

Israel wept and said: AND HIS JUDGEMENTS WERE FOR ISRAEL (ibid.).

And they all said (Yeshayahu 57:2): LET PEACE COME AND REST IN THEIR ABODE (Devarim Rabbah 7 and 11; Yalkut Shimoni, Parashas Vayelech; Midrash Tanchuma; Divrei ha-Yamim shel Moshe Rabbenu).

AND HE BURIED HIM IN THE VALLEY (Devarim 34:6) — How did Moshe merit that God should deal with him [i.e., his burial]? When Israel was engaged in gathering the spoils of Egypt, he [Moshe] went through the city for three days and three nights to find Yosef's coffin, but he could not discover its whereabouts. After he had expended much effort, he met Serach, the daughter of Asher, who asked him: "Moshe, our master, why do you exert yourself so greatly?"

He answered: "I am looking for the coffin of Yosef, but I cannot find it."

She said to him: "Come with me." She led him to the Nile and said: "In this place they made a coffin of lead weighing five hundred kikar and they placed him inside of it. They then sealed it and cast it into the river, for Pharoah's magicians had told him, 'Do you wish to insure that this people not leave your dominion? Make sure that they do not find Yosef's coffin and they will never leave here, for he had made them swear accordingly [that they would not leave Egypt without taking his remains with them].'"

Moshe immediately stood by the riverbank and said: "Yosef, Yosef! You know that you made Israel swear that when God took them out [they would take your remains with them]. Accord honor to the God of Israel and do not cause Israel's redemption to be delayed. You have good deeds — plead for mercy before your Creator and rise from the depths!"

Immediately, the coffin began to ascend and came up from the depths at one time. He [Moshe] took it on his shoulder and carried it, while all of Israel followed him, carrying their silver and gold.

God then said to him: "If the kindness that you have done is inconsequential in your eyes — in My eyes it is great, for you paid no heed to the silver and gold. I too will descend Myself, and act with kindness towards you when you pass from this world" (*Yalkut Shimoni*, end of *Vezos ha-Berachah*).

CUSTOMS OF THE SEVENTH OF ADAR

✿ It is customary, in many Jewish communities, for the *Chevrah Kadisha* [the burial society] to observe the seventh of Adar as a day of gathering for all of its members. On this day they hold a festive banquet with the participation of the entire community. Officers of the *Chevrah* are chosen and regulations adopted. The day is considered as a festival for them and for the community. Why was the seventh day of Adar chosen as the holiday of the *Chevrah Kadisha?*

The reason for this custom reflects praise upon Israel and upon those who are engaged in the practice of mitzvos. Men of all occupations are happy when they have a lot of work and are sad when there is little work. In the case of the members of the *Chevrah Kadisha*, however, although their work calls for them to perform kindness for both the dead and the living — work which they perform faithfully — they never rejoice in their work. When are they happy? When their work ceases.

The only time when we find that the work of those who perform kindness for the dead ceased was on the seventh of Adar, the day when Moshe died. No mortal engaged in his burial — only God Himself.

Alternatively, the seventh of Adar was chosen as the day of gathering for those who perform kindness for the dead because this date never falls on Shabbos.

THE EXTENT OF DIVINE JUDGEMENT

Come and see how exactingly and precisely God acts with the righteous, and how severe is the curse uttered by a Sage. From whom can this be seen? From Moshe, for when Israel sinned with the golden calf, the Divine wrath would have come upon them had it not been for the plea of mercy that Moshe, God's elect, made for them. He endangered himself because of Israel, and said to God: AND NOW IF YOU WILL BEAR THEIR SIN. AND IF NOT ERASE ME PLEASE FROM THE BOOK THAT YOU HAVE WRITTEN (*Shemos* 32:32).

The Midrash says: The curse of a Sage — even if issued conditionally — comes about. From where can this be seen? From Moshe, who said: ERASE ME. Even though the sin of the golden calf was atoned for, Moshe's name was erased from the Torah portion of *Tetzaveh*, where it is not mentioned at all (*Rabbenu Bachya*).

And why was Moshe's name erased specifically from the portion of *Tetzaveh*? Because in most years, this portion is read on the week during which the seventh of Adar, the anniversary of Moshe's death, falls (*Gra*).

Amalek

CHAPTER TWO

PARASHAS ZACHOR

On the Shabbos before Purim, two Torah scrolls are taken from the *aron kodesh*; the first is used for the regular weekly *sidrah*, with seven people called up for the reading, and the second is used for *maftir*. We read the portion of REMEMBER THAT WHICH AMALEK DID UNTO YOU from the *sidrah* of *Ki Setze* (*Devarim* 25:17-19). This Shabbos is referred to as *Shabbos Zachor* — remember — based on the *maftir* reading. The *haftarah* is read from the Book of *Shemuel* (I 15:1-34), which also speaks of Amalek.

🙠 All of Israel is obligated — as a positive Torah precept — to detest Amalek and his descendants and to verbally recall that nation's treachery. We are obliged to tell our children what Amalek did to us when we departed from Egypt. This mitzvah will only be completely fulfilled when Amalek's memory shall be totally obliterated and no remnant of that nation shall be extant. The Torah (*Devarim* 25:17-19) states: REMEMBER THAT WHICH AMALEK DID UNTO YOU, ON YOUR WAY AS YOU DEPARTED FROM EGYPT...YOU SHALL OBLITERATE THE MEMORY OF AMALEK, YOU SHALL NOT FORGET. Our Sages explained: YOU SHALL OBLITERATE THE MEMORY — i.e., verbally; YOU SHALL NOT FORGET — i.e., you shall harbor enmity in your heart.

🙠 So as to be able to fulfill these Torah precepts — i.e., verbally recounting Amalek's treachery and harboring enmity in one's heart — the Sages ordained that this portion be publicly read from a Torah scroll once a year on the Shabbos before Purim. This time was chosen so as to juxtapose the obliteration of Amalek to the obliteration of Haman who was a descendant of that nation.

⚘ Although this portion is read annually when the portion of *Ki Setze* is read in the summertime, it is nevertheless obligatory that it be read at the prescribed time before Purim. When the portion is read as part of the *sidrah* of *Ki Setze*, the intent is to fulfill our obligation of reading the Torah each Shabbos. When this portion is read on the Shabbos before Purim, our intent is to fulfill the obligation of obliterating the memory of Amalek.

⚘ Because the reading of this portion at the prescribed time is a positive precept, the Torah reader must have conscious intent to enable the congregation to fulfill their obligation through his reading, and the congregation must have conscious intent to fulfill their obligation by listening to the reader and considering this as if they had read the portion themselves.

⚘ Some authorities maintain that if one failed to hear this portion read on the Shabbos before Purim, one can fulfill the obligation to remember that which Amalek did by listening to the Torah portion that is read on Purim itself.

A minor who has not reached the age of bar mitzvah should not be called as *maftir* on *Shabbos Zachor*. Moreover, he should not read the portion publicly so as to allow others to fulfill their obligation by hearing his reading. Since he — as a minor — is not obligated in this *mitzvah*, he cannot enable others to fulfill their obligation through his reading. Some maintain that a minor should not be called as *maftir* for any of the four special Torah readings [*Zachor, Parah, Shekalim* and *ha-Chodesh*].

⚘ Women are not obligated to hear the portion of Amalek read; the fact that they come to the synagogues to hear the reading is a custom which they have accepted upon themselves. The mitzvah of remembering Amalek was addressed to the males, for the obligation of waging war to obliterate all remnants of Amalek is incumbent upon men alone. Since women are not obligated to wage war, they are not obligated in the mitzvah of remembering. Some authorities maintain, however, that women are obligated to hear the portion of *Zachor*, for the dispensation of women vis-a-vis waging war applies only to voluntary wars and not to wars which are a mitzvah.

⚓ Although we do not remove Torah scrolls from the synagogue to read the *sidrah* for a person who is ill and unable to leave his home, or for a person who is incarcerated, we do so for the reading of *Parashas Zachor* since this reading is a mitzvah. Some authorities maintain that this applies to the reading of *Parashas Parah* as well.

AMALEK

Amalek was the grandson of Esav; his father was Elifaz — Esav's oldest son — and his mother was Elifaz's concubine — Timna — a daughter of one of the princes of Seir.

Our Sages said: Timna was herself the illegitimate child of Elifaz. When she grew up, she sought to marry one of Avraham's grandchildren because of their reknown among the nations. She approached Yaakov, but he would not accept her because of her illegitimacy. She then approached Elifaz — her own father — and he took her as his concubine. Thus, Amalek — her son from Elifaz — was the illegitimate son born to an illegitimate mother.

Elifaz, Amalek's father, grew up in Yitzchak's home. He was circumcised at the age of eight days, for Esav circumcised all of his children as long as his father was still alive. Thus, Elifaz had a certain measure of decency about him. His son, Amalek, however, was born after Yitzchak died. He was therefore not circumcised, and he was raised in the atmosphere of the home of Esav. Amalek inherited his grandfather's hatred for Yaakov and for his descendants.

Esav told Amalek: "How I have strived to kill Yaakov — but I did not succeed. Resolve to exact vengeance for me!"

Amalek asked him: "How can I hope to prevail against them?"

Esav answered: "Let this tradition be yours. When you see them doing something wrong, that is the time to attack them."

Amalek lived for a long time. He witnessed Yaakov and his sons descend to Egypt, and he was still alive when they were redeemed two hundred and ten years later. When Amalek saw them enslaved in Egypt, he said to himself: "My grandfather's vengeance has been realized, for they will never be freed from their bondage. And even if they are set free, I will be waiting for them like a predatory bear and will annihilate them."

Amalek's descendants were many, and he instilled in their hearts his inexorable hatred for Yaakov. When Amalek saw the children of Israel marching out of Egypt, his animosity burst forth like a flame. He took his people and prepared an ambush. While Israel was weary and tired, Amalek attacked them, as the verse (*Shemos* 17:8) states: AND AMALEK CAME.

AMALEK'S HATRED FOR ISRAEL

Amalek's hatred for Israel is deep rooted and nothing comparable can be found among the other nations who have shown their animosity towards Israel. As regards the anti-Semites of other nations, one can find times when their animosity is unexpressed. Amalek's hatred, on the other hand, is unrelenting and they constantly plan our destruction. Other nations can be bribed or placated; Amalek is unwilling to be placated through any means. When other nations who sought to destroy Israel saw the hand of God punishing them, they immediately became frightened and submitted. Amalek did not flinch or hesitate. Though they witnessed God's wonders and miracles, though they saw Him exact vengeance on the enemies of His people and though they knew that they would be punished if they attacked Israel, they were not deterred. Their very essence is hatred for Israel, hatred that is expressed even if they have nothing to gain therefrom, hatred without cause or motive. It is hatred for the sake of hatred alone and it therefore never ceases.

When Avraham's sun began to rise and all of the world's peoples saw that the name of God was upon him, they realized that he was the source of their blessing and related to him as "a prince of God" in their midst. Avraham's greatness was manifested by his rejection of idolatry and by his becoming a servant of God alone. He instructed his sons and his household to follow in the path that he had charted — to act righteously and justly. Yishmael, his eldest son, refused to follow in his father's footsteps, but he laid no claim to being Avraham's successor and was content to leave the spiritual legacy of Avraham to his brother Yitzchak.

Esav was born to Yitzchak and lived a life full of every manner of spiritual abomination — including robbery, murder and liscentiousness. Nevertheless, Esav sought to be Yitzchak's heir in both the physical and spiritual worlds. When God ordained that these blessings be given to Yaakov alone — for Yaakov's life was pure and all of his actions reflected his holiness and love for his fellow man — Esav saw that his designs were not to be fulfilled, for both the birthright and the blessings had been given to Yaakov. He sulked and retired to the land of Seir, but did not despair of becoming his father's heir. Rather, he nurtured an eternal hatred for his brother — hatred based on jealousy — and he never stopped thinking that the inheritance of Yitzchak would eventually be his; through deceit if not by right.

Esav saw that he was unable to destroy Yaakov, for (Tehillim 121:4) THE GUARDIAN OF ISRAEL DOES NOT SLEEP OR SLUMBER. He commanded his children to exact his vengeance. Some of them despaired of being able to do so, for they said to themselves: "We shall never be able to prevail against the one whom the King of the world protects. Our own possessions are sufficient and we have no desire for the legacy of Avraham and Yitzchak — neither the obligations nor the rewards." They drew far away from the path of Avraham and Yitzchak, choosing lives of ever growing evil.

But there was one despicable member of Esav's family, an offspring who was himself from an abominable source, who approached his grandfather and said: "I am not frightened by God. I do not fear His awe. I feel no shame because of your deeds or because of my own. I will accord no honor to the acts of the righteous — I despise them and their actions. Greatness and strength are mine. I shall go forth and wage war against your brother's sons who have have inherited the greatness that is yours. I shall fight them openly and in ambush. I will slay those who stray behind and I shall slaughter their great ones, until I succeed in totally destroying all of them."

As long as there was a modicum of decency in Esav and his sons — a residue of the decency that had adhered to them from the homes of Avraham and Yitzchak — they had no desire to spoil the good and the splendor that existed in the world. But when this son was born who was the very incarnation of evil, then we find that AMALEK CAME AND WAGED WAR WITH ISRAEL (Shemos 17:8)..

Thus, in the future, all of the nations of the world are destined to abandon their evil ways and seek protection under the wings of the Shechinah. But Amalek — who has not a trace of decency — will never repent and shall pursue their path of evil until the very end. The verse (Shemos 17:16) therefore states: FOR THERE IS A HAND UPON THE THRONE OF GOD, A WAR OF GOD WITH AMALEK FROM GENERATION TO GENERATION.

THE FIRST AMONG NATIONS

Regarding Bil'am, the prophet of the nations, the verse (*Bemidbar* 24:20) states: AND HE SAW AMALEK AND HE DREW HIS PARABLE AND SAID, AMALEK IS THE FIRST AMONG NATIONS AND HIS END SHALL BE ETERNAL DEATH. Is Amalek "the first among nations"? Were they not preceded by the seventy nations descended from Shem, Ever and Cham? Rather, the verse should be understood in this sense: THE FIRST AMONG NATIONS to wage war against Israel was Amalek. From the time when Israel left Egypt, no nation dared attacked her until Amalek came.

THE NATIONS HEARD AND TREMBLED, FEAR GRIPPED THE RESIDENTS OF PHILLISTIA. THEN THE PRINCES OF EDOM WERE CONFUSED, THE MIGHTY ONES OF MOAV WERE SEIZED WITH SHIVERING, THE RESIDENTS OF CANAAN LOST THEIR RESOLVE. FEAR AND AWE FELL UPON THEM, THE GREATNESS OF YOUR ARM MADE THEM STILL LIKE A ROCK (*Shemos* 15:14-16).

When did all this transpire? When God manifested His signs and wonders in the land of Egypt and when He split the sea for Israel along with all of the waters of the world, all of humanity understood that God was performing miracles for His children, Israel. All that had been corrupted by man was about to be rectified, for God's glory was to be revealed on Mt. Sinai and the Torah was to be given to Israel, transforming them into a nation of *kohanim* who would serve on behalf of all of the nations of the world. They were to enter the chosen land and make it into AN ABODE FOR YOUR DWELLING, A SANCTUARY TO GOD, THE WORK OF YOUR HANDS (*Shemos* 15:17). It was to become the place where ALL NATIONS WOULD HURRY, AND MANY PEOPLE WILL GO THERE AND SAY: COME, LET US GO UP TO THE MOUNTAIN OF GOD, TO THE HOUSE OF THE GOD OF YAAKOV AND WE SHALL BE TAUGHT HIS WAYS AND WE SHALL FOLLOW HIS PATHS (*Yeshayahu* 2:2).

All the mighty kings of the world — with Pharaoh at their head

— trembled and feared, the residents of Phillistine and Canaan reconciled themselves that the land was to be returned to her rightful owner. The princes of Edom and the officers of Moav were powerless and their previous hatred for Israel was forgotten. All of humanity was ready to join Israel in the last declaration of her song: GOD SHALL REIGN FOREVER. Who was so foolhardy as to wage war with Israel at this hour, for does one wage war when there is no hope of victory!?

But what did Amalek do at this time? AND AMALEK CAME AND WAGED WAR WITH ISRAEL. Was she mightier than Pharaoh, stronger than Sichon and Og, than the thirty-one kings of the land of Canaan, than the princes of Edom and the officers of Moav!?

Why did she choose to wage war at a time when every other nation was prepared to surrender? Had Israel crossed her borders in the past, or did she threaten to do so in the future? No, for Israel had kept a distance of four hundred *parsah*, in addition to the five other nations who dwelled between Amalek and the awesome wilderness, bereft of water and bread, in which Israel encamped.

Amalek's cruel, serpent-like character led them to attack Israel. They knew that their actions would cause them to be eternally uprooted from the world, but they did not hesitate to attempt to extinguish the flame of the awareness of God's wonders which burned in all of mankind. They sought to sow confusion and doubt in the hearts of Israel and the nations.

Therefore, you Israel must mete out to them what the Amalekim sought to do to you. Their hatred brought them to the point where they were prepared to commit suicide if only to allow it to be expressed. You too must hate them and YOU SHALL OBLITERATE THE MEMORY OF AMALEK, YOU SHALL NOT FORGET!

Israel is referred to as THE FIRST, as the verse states: ISRAEL IS SANCTIFIED TO GOD, THE FIRST OF HIS PRODUCE (*Yirmeyahu* 2:3). In contrast, Amalek is also referred to as the first, as the verse states: THE FIRST AMONG NATIONS IS AMALEK (*Bemidbar* 24:20). What does this teach us?

The Sages explained: The essence of any object is referred to as its first part or its *terumah*. Just as there is *terumah* in the pure essence of an object, so too is there *terumah* in the impure essence of an object.

The essence of all that is pure and sanctified in this world is to be found in Israel. In contrast, the essence of all corruption and impurity in this world — the base defilement which has its root in the primordial serpent — is personified by Amalek. Therefore, Amalek is also referred to as the "first".

Thus, Israel stands on one side as the root of all holiness, while Amalek stands opposite her, as the root of all corruption. The other nations of the world stand between them. When Israel is spiritually weak, the scales tip towards Amalek and her influence prevails, sinking the world into a state of moral deprivation and decay. However, despite Israel's weakness, Amalek is unable to totally destroy her.

In the future, when Israel's spiritual state shall be mighty, she shall incline the entire world towards the side of good. Amalek alone — whose essence is totally evil and corrupt — shall lose their capacity to exist, and their memory will be obliterated from beneath the heavens.

AND AMALEK CAME

The Sages explained: The Amalek mentioned in the verse refers to Amalek, the son of Elifaz — he who was raised in Esav's home. He was still alive at this time and came at the head of his nation to wage war on Israel (*Mechilta, Parashas Beshalach*).

AND AMALEK CAME — i.e., he came with a strategy. He gathered all of the nations and said to them: "Come and help me wage war with Israel."

They told him: "We will be unable to stand up to them, for Pharoah sought to do battle with them, and he and his armies were drowned in the sea! How can we stand up against them?"

Amalek replied: "I shall advise you as to what you should do. If they are victorious, then flee. But if not, come and join me against Israel" (*Yalkut Shimoni, Parashas Beshalach* 262).

AND AMALEK CAME — R. Nasan said: Amalek came from the land of Seir. He travelled four handred *parsah* so as to wage war with Israel.

The verse states: AND HE [ESAV] WENT TO HIS LAND BECAUSE OF HIS BROTHER YAAKOV(*Bereshis* 36:6). He went because of the debt that Yitzchak's descendants were required to pay — the debt of (ibid. 15:13) YOUR CHILDREN SHALL BE STRANGERS IN A LAND THAT IS NOT THEIRS. Esav said: "I shall leave this land, for I have no part in the gift which this land represents and therefore am not required to pay the debt which accompanies that gift." He also left because of his shame for having sold his birthright to Yaakov. His grandson Amalek waited until the children of Israel left Egypt, which showed that the debt of AND THEY SHALL SUBJUGATE THEM AND AFFLICT THEM (ibid.) had been paid, and immediately attacked them (*Chizkuni*).

What did Amalek do to them? He went to the archive rooms of the Egyptians and removed the records on which the names of the tribes of Israel had been inscribed. He then stood outside the cloud that protected the camp of the children of Israel and called out: "Reuven, Shimon, we are your brothers. Come out, for we wish to do business with you." When one of them would emerge, Amalek would immediately kill him (*Yalkut Shimoni, Parashas Ki Setze* 938).

Amalek was always a scourge to Israel. When Israel came to Refidim, before the Torah was given, and asked IS GOD AMONG US OR NOT (*Shemos* 17:7), it was then that AMALEK CAME and attacked them. When the spies were sent, we find that AMALEK DESCENDED...AND SMOTE THEM UNTIL CHORMAH (*Bemidbar* 14:45). When Amalek learned that Aharon had died, and the cloud which had protected Israel dissipated, the verse states: THE CANAANI, THE KING OF ARAD HEARD (ibid. 21:1). Our Sages explained that this refers to the people of Amalek, who masqueraded as Canaanites, pretending to join Israel in their mourning, but then attacking them. In later generations, when the Babylonians came to besiege Israel, Amalek came and stood by the side, saying, "If Israel prevails, we will claim that we have come to help them. And if the Babylonians prevail, we will turn against Israel and destroy them" (*Yalkut Shimoni, Parashas Chukas* 864).

THE SOURCE OF AMALEK'S STRENGTH

Where did Amalek draw the strength to attack Israel at a time when they were under the wings of the *Shechinah* and enveloped in the cloud that protected them? Our Sages explained: The verse states, AND THEY WAGED WAR WITH ISRAEL AT REFIDIM (*Shemos* 17:8). [The word Refidim can be seen as an acronym for *rafu yedayhem* — their hands became weakened; i.e., they stopped occupying themselves with the Torah.] CAN THE REED SHOOT UP IF NOT IN A SWAMP? CAN THE GRASS FLOURISH WITHOUT WATER? (*Iyov* 8:11). Similarly, can Israel survive if they do not occupy themselves with the Torah? Because Israel forsook the path of the Torah, their enemies were able to attack them, for their adversaries are only able to attack when Israel sins and transgresses (*Yalkut Shimoni, Parashas Beshalach* 262).

REFIDIM

Amalek was loyal to the legacy of his grandfather, Esav, who had instructed him: "Let this tradition be yours. When you see them [Israel] doing something wrong, that is the time to attack them."

What had Israel done wrong when they encamped at Refidim?

When Israel emerged from the sea and entered the wilderness of Shur, they knew that they were approaching the mountain of God to receive the Torah. They were about to become a KINGDOM OF KOHANIM AND A HOLY NATION (*Shemos* 19:6) — a people whose survival was no longer to be dependent upon bread alone or whose thirst was to be quenched solely by springs of water. Their viability was to be dependent upon their fealty to the word of God. In the desert — bereft of sources of food and drink — they were to place their trust in God, for He would not leave them to starve and die.

They entered the wilderness of Shur, and for three days — as long as they still had strength — they neither complained nor murmured, accepting their travails with equanimity and trust in God. They understood that the Torah which they were about to receive could only be acquired through affliction; that by discarding sensual pleasures and seeking delight in God alone, they would merit, in the end, the pleasures of the physical world as well. The entire people, some three million men, women and children, stood ready to to receive the Torah and accept the yoke of its responsibilities — despite the difficulties — upon themselves.

When the people ca▮▮▮arah and found water there, they were faced with a ▮▮▮▮D THEY COULD NOT DRINK THE WATERS AT MARAH BECAUSE THEY WERE BITTER (*Shemos* 15:23). Their spirit temporarily failed them, as the verse (ibid. 15:24) states: AND THE PEOPLE COMPLAINED TO MOSHE. The verse specifies that it was the people who complained, not the elders and scholars. Moreover, their complaint was minor: WHAT SHALL WE DRINK (ibid.)? They had weathered their first crisis.

The Torah proceeds to inform us: AND THEY CAME TO EILIM AND THERE WERE TWELVE SPRINGS OF WATER AND SEVENTY PALM TREES, AND THEY CAMPED THERE BY THE WATER (ibid. 15:27). They still had bread with them from Egypt, but after three days, they had run out of water. They were therefore overjoyed to find the springs at Eilim, as the verse points out, THEY CAMPED THERE BY THE WATER.

But they were not to completely satiate themselves with these waters, for they immediately set out into the desert of Sinai. They still had water with them, but now their bread ran out, and they wondered: "How can an entire nation live for a single day without bread? In the end," they told themselves, "God will provide us with bread. But why does He drive us to the point of starvation? If this is the life that the Torah demands, it is doubtful whether the nation will be able to stand up to these constant tests." Thus, the verse (ibid. 16:2) states, regarding this crisis: AND THE ENTIRE CONGREGATION COMPLAINED TO MOSHE AND TO AHARON IN THE WILDERNESS.

When they were first tested in the wilderness of Shur, the entire nation passed and showed their faith and trust in God. At the crisis at Marah, the common people complained, but the elders and wise men remained steadfast. Now when the third test occurred in the desert, the faith of the entire people began to waver. Their trial seemed to be beyond endurance. If these tests and crises were to be a constant part of the life of the nation, it was clear that the path they had chosen would be too difficult for an entire nation to follow.

Nevertheless, their request and their complaints were still within the realm of propriety, for they asked for nothing more than bread and water.

The manna descended and their bread was provided — even though it was only sufficient for a single day — and the people were calmed. They were ready to receive the Torah and follow its path knowing that their daily needs were to be provided. But, the water which they had taken with them from the springs at Eilim ran out.

Now they were again tested by thirst, as the Torah tells us: AND THEY ENCAMPED AT REFIDIM AND THERE WAS NO WATER FOR THE PEOPLE TO DRINK. AND THE PEOPLE QUARRELLED WITH MOSHE (Shemos 17:1-2). Though the entire nation had previously complained, not all of them had joined in the quarrel.

The tests to which they were being subjected seemed to be beyond endurance. They had begun their journey with the bread that they had hastily prepared as they left Egypt, but without water. They had then found water, but it was too bitter to drink. When they found water that they could drink, they lacked bread. When the manna fell and provided them with bread, they again found themselves without water. It seemed that whenever they had one, they lacked the other. Was this to be symptomatic of the Torah way of life?

AND THEY CAMPED AT REFIDIM — the Sages explained: Their hands became weak from the Torah [Refidim can be seen as an acronym for rafu yedayhem — their hands became weakened; i.e., they stopped occupying themselves with the Torah]. Some members of the nation began to despair of ever being able to bear the yoke of the Torah under such constantly difficult conditions.

MASAH AND MERIVAH

AND HE CALLED THE PLACE BY THE NAME MASAH [TESTING] AND ME-
RIVAH [QUARREL] BECAUSE OF THE QUARREL OF THE CHILDREN OF
ISRAEL AND BECAUSE OF THEIR TEST OF GOD WHEN THEY SAID: IS
GOD IN OUR MIDST OR NOT? (*Shemos* 17:7).

How is it possible that the holy nation of Israel, having witnessed God's miracles and wonders on a daily basis, would pose
a question of this sort? What was the "quarrel" that occurred
there?

R. Yehudah, R. Nechemyah and the Sages all offered their opin-
ions.

R. Yehudah explained: They said, "If He is Master over all of existence like He is master over us, then we shall serve Him. But
if not, we shall rebel against Him."

R. Nechemyah explained: They said, "If He provides sustenance
like a king who is aware of the needs of His people but whose
people are not dependent upon Him, then we shall serve Him.
But if not, then we shall rebel against Him."

The Sages explained: [The people said,] "If He knows what our
thoughts are, then we shall serve Him. But if not, we shall rebel
against Him."

The Holy One, blessed is He, said: "If you seek to examine Me,
then let the wicked one come and examine you!" Immediately
we find that AMALEK CAME AND WAGED WAR WITH ISRAEL
(*Shemos Rabbah* 24).

According to R. Yehudah's explanation, Israel revealed that
they were willing to accept the yoke of the Torah — no matter
how difficult it might be — provided that this path and the
conduct, as it were, of God would be true of all nations. They
were not prepared to accept that they were to be singled out to
face travails more bitter than those facing other nations.

R. Nechemyah added that Israel was prepared to be treated differently than other nations in that their sustenance would be granted them directly from the King's home and would not be a result of their own efforts. They asked only that they not be forced to constantly plead for its provision.

The Sages expanded this and explained that Israel was prepared to live under more difficult conditions than other nations, and was even willing to be put into the position wherein they would be called upon to plead for their sustenance constantly rather than having it provided for them in a natural manner. They asked only that their personal failures not be seen as being grounds for denying them life. No man can always control himself. Circumstances can lead him to quarrel and complain — as they were doing now. They therefore predicated their acceptance of the yoke of the Torah on God's being aware of their inner thoughts and needs. They said: "If He will show that He is aware of man's inner thoughts by granting him his needs before he reaches the point of death, we are prepared to follow His path. But if He will not evidence this awareness, and will grant our needs only when we have reached the point of death, then we are not willing to accept the yoke of His rule, for we shall be unable to always endure such hardship and will surely rebel against Him."

They did not despair of being able to accept the Torah; they only showed that their hands were weak by establishing conditions — conditions which they felt were necessary if they were to be able to live in accordance with its demands.

God said to them: "You establish conditions for me? You seek to examine Me? You fear that I shall make demands of you that you will be unable to fulfill? Let Amalek come and examine you and establish whether you have followed Me in all the ways that are within your abilities."

IDOLATRY IN THE CAMP OF ISRAEL

YOU FOLLOWED ME IN THE WILDERNESS IN A LAND THAT WAS NOT PLANTED (*Yirmeyahu* 2:2) — The Sages explained: This [the complete dependence on God that characterized Israel's existence in the desert] is only temporary and will only last as long as you are on the way [to the Land of Israel] and until the Torah is permanently implanted within you. Afterwards, you shall enter the land which is My palace, and you will plant at the time of planting, sow at the time of sowing, and harvest at the time of harvesting, and I shall grant you bounty greater than any other nation or land.

However, the imperative to remove all traces of idolatry and serve God alone — this is incumbent upon you now and for generations to come. Have you removed the foreign gods from your midst? Have you brought yourselves under My wing and shattered all of your idols? Let Amalek come and examine you. If your hearts are completely with Me, you have nothing to fear. But if there is among you a man or woman whose soul still clings to the idols of Egypt and their abominations, let them [the idols] come and save you from the wicked Amalek! The verse therefore states: AND AMALEK CAME (*Shemos* 17:8) ... AND HE TAILED AFTER YOU [STRIKING] ALL THOSE WHO WERE WEAK (*Devarim* 25:18).

AND HE TAILED AFTER THEM — R. Nachman explained: All those whom the "protective cloud" cast out were caught by Amalek. The Sages explained: This refers to the tribe of Dan who were cast out by the "protective cloud" because they were all idol worshippers. The idol which Michah had created was in their midst, and there were many among them who had not wholeheartedly resolved to serve God alone (*Yalkut Shimoni, Parashas Ki Setze*).

[God said to them:] "I restrain My anger when you fail to accomplish what you are capable of accomplishing. And you worry that I might command you to do something of which you are not capable! Let Amalek come and examine you."

AND HE TAILED AFTER YOU — Amalek was like a fly which hovers over any place where it finds an open wound. When Amalek found a weak link in Israel, they came and waged war with Israel.

Sin and transgression — these are Amalek's strengths. Amalek is the cause of sin and through Amalek punishment is meted out. This is the manner in which Satan acts. He first creates a stumbling block for man, ascends to God and accuses them and then descends to carry out their destruction.

REMEMBER THAT WHICH AMALEK DID TO YOU

ASHER KARCHA (*Devarim* 25:18) [literally, he happened upon you] — i.e., he rendered you impure. This is similar to what the verse (ibid. 23:11) says, AND WHEN THERE IS A MAN AMONG YOU WHO IS NOT PURE BECAUSE OF A HAPPENING [i.e., a seminal emission] AT NIGHT.

The Sages explained: KARCHA — he cooled you off [from the root *kar*] for the other nations of the world. To what can this be compared? To a boiling basin which no one could enter. A worthless person came along and jumped into it. Even though he was scalded, he cooled it off for others. Similarly, when Israel came out of Egypt, all of the nations of the world feared them, as the verse states, THEN THE PRINCES OF EDOM WERE CONFUSED ...FEAR AND TREPIDATION FELL UPON THEM (*Shemos* 15:15-16). But when Amalek came and engaged them in battle — though he was punished by their hands — he cooled them off [i.e., made them less awe-inspiring] to the other nations of the world. (*Yalkut Shimoni, Parashas Ki Setze* 938).

Before the sun of Avraham began to rise, the entire world was desolate. It was as if the light of the world had been extinguished and the world was destined to sink into an abyss of corruption, evil and paganism. And then Avraham came and lit an ember. His children followed and fanned that ember into a mighty flame that gave light and warmth. When Israel left Egypt, they did so through spectacular wonders and a revelation of the *Shechinah*. All of Israel, all of Egypt and all the peoples of the world realized that God alone rules and there is none beside Him. The entire universe waited expectantly for that exalted occasion when God would descend to Mt. Sinai and speak directly to man. Man's pride was about to be humbled and God alone would remain exalted. God had revealed Himself to His entire people and designated them to be His emissaries to all other nations; to raise the level of every nation and kingdom and illuminate a path for them. Would there still be a nation audacious enough to contend, WHO IS GOD THAT I SHOULD LISTEN TO HIM (*Shemos* 5:2)?

All of Israel was prepared for this occasion, and they were also prepared to bring the peoples of the world close to Him as will be in the end of days. And then this wicked nation, Amalek, came and ruined everything. He leaped into the fire — a fire which all others feared — and was scalded, but he cooled the fire for everyone else. And now, what did the other nations contend? They said: "The battle continues. We have only surrendered temporarily." The rectification of the world would again be postponed for many years — until the end of time.

And as for Israel; though they saw that Amalek had been scalded, they too found their fire and the strength of their faith cooled and they began to complain and quarrel with God. Who would have believed that there was a nation with the audacity to try to wage war with them after all that had transpired — yet Amalek came and did so!

The battle continued. Israel had not yet lost her fear of mortal man, replacing it with fear of God's majesty and grandeur. Amalek attacked the weak elements. He instilled fear in the minds of those whose hands were slipping as they held the yoke of Divine responsibility, and he planted anxiety in the hearts of those who were strong.

When they stood at Mt. Sinai, after waging war with Amalek, something was missing inside of them. This slight failing later manifested itself in a series of mistakes and misdeeds. Israel's rectification, and the resultant restoration of the world to its intended course, was postponed.

For more than 3,000 years the final redemption has not come. The world still hovers over an abyss — all because of this vile serpent: Amalek, the wicked, may his name and memory be obliterated.

AND IT SHALL BE WHEN GOD GRANTS YOU RESPITE

HE PERFORMS WONDERS WHICH ARE BEYOND EXAMINATION (*Iyov* 9:10) — Is there anything which is impossible for Him? Could He not have subjugated Amalek so that they dare not attack Israel then? Could He not have paralyzed them with fear as He did to the other nations?

There is a reason why He acted as He did. The subjugation of the nations to God's will is a source of merit for them. AND EGYPT SHALL KNOW THAT I AM GOD (*Shemos* 14:4) — Egypt's realization that there is a God is a source of merit. Similarly, when Phillistine and Moav humbled themselves before the majesty of God, they served as instruments — perhaps unwillingly —

for the revelation of God's sovereignty over the world. The merit of having served as instruments of God will enable them to share in the reward due Israel at the end of days.

Amalek, however, is totally devoid of good. It is not for them, or for those like them, to serve as instruments that establish God's sovereignty. God therefore removed all vestiges of fear from Amalek's heart so that they might remain eternally distanced from Him.

AND IT WILL BE WHEN GOD, YOUR LORD, SHALL GRANT YOU RESPITE FROM ALL OF YOUR ENEMIES WHO SURROUND YOU (*Devarim* 25:19) — at the time when there shall no longer be any fear of war, when the fear of Amalek will vanish and nothing will stand in the way of the world submitting itself to God, then YOU SHALL DESTROY THE MEMORY OF AMALEK FROM BENEATH HEAVEN (ibid.). It will be as if Amalek had never existed — not them nor their wickedness. A world will exist which is whole and rectified like a new creation — a world without Amalek.

HATRED AS A MITZVAH

Until the time when God will grant us respite from our enemies and transform them into our friends, the only nation which we are obligated to hate is Amalek. The Torah itself — though it is entirely kindness and mercy — obligates us to hate Amalek and wage war with them, collectively and individually. We are to do battle with the pollution and corruption which they instilled in all nations, as well as with the defilement which they infected us with — i.e., our willingness to subjugate ourselves to wills other than that of God alone.

Ours is a war of annihilation against Amalek — not an attempt to subjugate them or capture their territory. We seek neither benefit nor pleasure from them nor from anything which is theirs. We seek to destroy them along with their property, and we shall not touch their booty.

As long as we are unable to totally obliterate Amalek, we are to hate them unrelentingly, for that hatred is itself part of their destruction. We are dutybound to distance ourselves from the evil that Amalek represents, and there is no greater distance than that engendered by eternal enmity. We are obliged to drive out all vestiges of Amalek's wickedness from our hearts and from the hearts of all mankind. The greater our animosity towards Amalek, the greater is our love for God and our commitment to His service.

EXCERPTS FROM THE COMMENTARIES ABOUT AMALEK

The evil one [i.e., Satan], who is seen and unseen, who waits by the crossroads travelled by all who serve God, placing obstacles and interfering with their pure faith — this is the root of Amalek. Whenever Israel neglects their service of God even for a moment, the strength of that wicked one increases. Everyone must therefore guard himself against sinning so as to weaken the powers of Amalek.

GOD IS AT WAR WITH AMALEK IN EVERY GENERATION (*Shemos* 17:16) — In every generation, God has reserved specific revelations of His light which are necessary to meet the needs of that specific generation. Only Amalek stands as an obstacle before these revelations, and God therefore abhors them for they cause His goodness to be withheld. Hence, every servant of God who seeks to have this Divine light revealed, and fails to merit this light because of Amalek's effect, must become Amalek's implacable enemy.

Amalek's strength is manifested only when man is oppressed by his worldly needs; they have no power when man enjoys spiritual serenity and is free from the search for sustenance. The verse (*Devarim* 25:19) therefore states: AND IT WILL BE WHEN GOD, YOUR LORD, SHALL GRANT YOU RESPITE FROM ALL OF YOUR ENE-MIES WHO SURROUND YOU, YOU SHALL DESTROY THE MEMORY OF AMALEK FROM BENEATH THE HEAVEN. When man enjoys spiritual serenity, he sees the utter worthlessness of evil. It is for this reason that the portion of *Zachor* is read on a Shabbos, for as the day of rest, it is most suited for uprooting Amalek from within one's soul. Similarly, the celebration of the miracle of Purim — when Israel overcame Haman, the descendant of Amalek — was set for a day when THEY RESTED FROM THEIR ENEMIES (*Esther* 9:16), rather than on the day of victory itself. It is the rest after the victory which completes the obliteration of Amalek's memory.

The complete obliteration of Amalek's memory will occur before the final redemption which will take place in the month of Nisan. It is therefore fitting that the reading of the portion of *Zachor* be scheduled during the days that precede Nisan.

Rosh Chodesh Nisan begins the new year for kings; i.e., the year of their reign is calculated from Nisan. The sovereignty of the kings of Israel is dependent upon the tangibility of the kingdom of Heaven. For this reason, the mitzvah of appointing a king over Israel is juxtaposed to the mitzvah of destroying Amalek.

THE DAY OF TURYANUS

The twelfth of Adar is recorded in *Megillas Ta'anis* as the anniversary of the date when God exacted His vengeance from one of Israel's bitter enemies. This was accomplished through two righteous brothers — Lilianus and Papus — who gave their lives in sanctification of God's name so as to save their brethren. The day was designated as a time of rejoicing on which there was to be no fasting and no eulogies were to be delivered. Later, the celebration on this date was annulled, because two other righteous brothers — Shmaya and Achiyah — were slain on this day.

Turyanus was a Roman procurator who harshly persecuted the Jews. One day, his daughter was discovered dead in the city of Lod, but the identity of her killer was not known. Turyanos declared: "The only enemies that I have here are the Jews. They must have killed her." He therefore decreed that all of the Jews in the area were to be put to death.

Two righteous brothers who lived in Lod, Lilianus and Papus, came forward and told Turyanus: "We are the ones who killed your daughter and her blood is on our heads."

Turyanus was well aware of the fact that they had not killed her and that their motive in confessing was only to save their brethren. Nevertheless, he accepted their confession and was prevented from taking revenge upon all of the Jews.

When Lulianus and Papus were brought out to be killed, Turyanus taunted them and said: "If you are of the same people as Chananyah, Mishael and Azaryah, let your God come and save you from my hand as He saved them from the hand of Nevuchadnezer."

They replied: "Chananyah, Mishael and Azaryah were righteous men who were worthy of having a miracle performed for them. Moreover, Nevuchadnezer was an eminent king who was worthy of having a miracle performed through him. But this wicked one [Turyanus] is nothing more than a commoner, and is unworthy of being the vehicle for a miracle. As for us, we have been condemned to death before God, and if you do not kill us, He has many executioners and many lions and bears who will strike us down and kill us. He has only delivered us to you so that He might later exact retribution for our blood from you!"

Despite what they had said, Turyanus had them executed.

It is told that while they were still gathered at the site of the execution, two men — who appeared to be high government officials — came and brutally murdered Turyanus. The final words of Lilianus and Papus were fulfilled: "God has only delivered us to you so that He might later exact retribution for our blood from you."

This episode occurred on the twelfth of Adar, and the date was designated as the day on which a miracle had occurred and was henceforth referred to as "the day of Turyanus."

The two brothers, Lilianus and Papus, are often anonymously referred to in Talmudic literature as "those slain in Lod." Thus, we find: No one can stand in the place of "the slain of Lod" in Gan Eden [i.e., no one is as worthy as they].

There is no record regarding what happened to the brothers Shmayah and Achiyah who were also killed on this day.

Purim

A DAY OF MOBILIZATION — A DAY OF FASTING ❖ THE
FAST OF ESTHER ❖ THE HALF-*SHEKEL* ❖ THE DAY OF
NIKANOR ❖ THE DAYS OF PURIM ❖ THE OBLIGATIONS
OF THE DAY ❖ THE THREE DAY PURIM ❖ THE READING
OF THE *MEGILLAH* ❖ THE *BERACHOS* RECITED ON THE
MEGILLAH ❖ EXCERPTS FROM THE COMMENTARIES ON
THE *MEGILLAH* ❖ HAMAN'S LETTER TO THE NATIONS —
WRITTEN IN THE NAME OF ACHASHVEROSH ❖ HAMAN
AND THE SCHOOLCHILDREN ❖ THREE VERSES — THREE
WARS ❖ THE CALL OF THE SHEEP ❖ MORDECHAI'S
PRAYER ❖ ESTHER'S PRAYER ❖ ESTHER ENTERS THE
INNER COURTYARD ❖ ZERESH'S ADVICE ❖ HAMAN'S
SCAFFOLD ❖ THE KING'S SLEEP WAS DISTURBED ❖
ACHASHVEROSH'S DREAM AND ITS INTERPRETATION ❖
FEASTING AND REJOICING ❖ THE SIGNIFICANCE OF THE
FESTIVE PURIM MEAL ❖ UNTIL HE CANNOT
DIFFERENTIATE ❖ WHY WE WEAR DISGUISES ON
PURIM ❖ *AL HA-NISIM* ❖ GIFTS FOR THE POOR ❖
EXCHANGING GIFTS OF FOOD BETWEEN FRIENDS ❖
LOVE AND UNITY — THE SHIELD AGAINST AMALEK ❖
HUMILITY AND GRATITUDE ❖ YOM KIPPUR — A DAY
LIKE PURIM ❖ PURIM AND THE *MEGILLAH* WILL NEVER
BE ABOLISHED

CHAPTER THREE

A DAY OF MOBILIZATION — A DAY OF FASTING

The thirteenth of Adar — *Ta'anis Esther* — is observed as a fast day in commemoration of the fast observed by Mordechai, Esther and all of Israel. On the thirteenth of Adar, the enemies of the Jews had planned to subjugate and destroy them, but THE OPPOSITE OCCURRED, AND THE JEWS HELD DOMINION OVER THEIR ENEMIES. THE JEWS GATHERED IN THEIR CITIES... (*Esther* 9:1-2).

Whenever they were faced with war, the Jews would fast. Thus, we find that Moshe fasted before he entered into battle with Amalek. The reason for such fasts is to affirm that man does not prevail because of his physical strength or prowess, but only when he lifts his eyes in prayer to heaven so that he might be granted Divine mercy to succeed. This was the purpose of the fast observed by Israel at the time of Haman as they gathered to defend themselves from those who sought to destroy them. To remember that fast, an annual fast was established on the day on which the Jews had gathered to defend themselves. Through this fast we recall that God sees and hears the prayers of each person at the time of his trouble.

The acceptance of this fast on the thirteenth of Adar is alluded to in the *Megillah*, for the verse states: AS THEY HAD ACCEPTED UPON THEMSELVES AND UPON THEIR DESCENDANTS, THESE FORMS OF FASTING AND SUPPLICATION (ibid. 9:31).

The fast is referred to as the Fast of Esther, for it was she who had first requested that the people fast, as the verse states: GO AND GATHER ALL OF THE JEWS WHO ARE IN SHUSHAN AND FAST ON MY BEHALF. DO NOT DRINK AND DO NOT EAT FOR THREE DAYS —

NEITHER BY NIGHT NOR BY DAY. MY MAIDENS AND I WILL ALSO FAST IN THIS MANNER (ibid. 4:16).

Our fast is not observed for three days as was the case with this original fast. Moreover, Esther's original fast was on the thirteenth, fourteenth and fifteenth of Nisan — for that was when Mordechai learned about Haman's intentions and about the royal letter written on the thirteenth of Nisan which called for the destruction of the Jews. Our fast is observed on the thirteenth of Adar, to commemorate the fast of the Jews who had gathered to defend themselves. Because Esther had proposed the first fast to deal with the pending calamity, all of the subsequent fasts decreed during that period are referred to by her name.

Some maintain that our fast on the thirteenth of Adar does indeed commemorate Esther's three day fast. However, since the annual fast could not be held in Nisan — for fasting is prohibited in that month — the Sages designated that it be held on the thirteenth of Adar which had been decreed a day of fasting when the Jews gathered to defend themselves. Although Esther's fast was three days long, the Sages were lenient and decreed that the commemorative fast last only one day.

THE FAST OF ESTHER

❧ The Fast of Esther is not specifically mentioned as one of the four public fasts ordained by the prophets. Consequently, we are more lenient in its observance; pregnant women, nursing mothers and those who are weak are not required to observe it. The *aneinu* prayer in *Shemoneh Esreh,* as well as the special Torah reading for fast days, are required on the Fast of Esther.

❧ If the thirteenth of Adar falls on Shabbos, the fast is observed on the preceding Thursday — the eleventh of Adar. Because Purim falls on the fourteenth, we do not put off the fast for the following day [as is the case, for example, when *Tishah b'Av* falls on Shabbos], nor do we observe it on Friday out of deference to Shabbos. [The only time when we fast on a Friday is when the fast day actually occurs on that day; e.g., the fast of *Asarah b'Teves.*] *Tachanun* is not said at *Minchah* on the Fast of Esther. Some people have a custom of wearing their Shabbos clothing at *Minchah* on the Fast of Esther, since the *Megillah* reading follows immediately afterwards.

THE HALF-*SHEKEL*

✿ It is customary to give three halves of the coins which serve as the local currency at *Minchah* on the thirteenth of Adar. This money is turned over to the poor who may use it in any manner which they see fit. This custom serves to remind us of the half-*shekel*s which Israel would donate at the time when the *Beis ha-Mikdash* was standing. The collection of this half- *shekel* was announced on *Rosh Chodesh* Adar.

✿ This commemorative act is performed before the reading of the *Megillah,* since all of Israel gathers in the synagogues to hear the *Megillah* reading. The half-*shekel* should be given before *Minchah,* for the diligent perform mitzvos as early as possible. Those who reside in cities which were not enclosed by walls give the half-*shekel* before the *Megillah* reading on the evening of the fourteenth of Adar. Those who live in Jerusalem [which was enclosed by walls at the time of the conquest of the Land of Israel by Yehoshua] give the half-*shekel* before the reading of the *Megillah* on the evening of the fifteenth of Adar.

✿ In a country where there is no coin which is referred to as being half of the local currency, it is customary for the synagogue wardens to provide three halves of coins issued elsewhere. These coins are acquired by the members of the congregation who use them to fulfill the custom of giving the half-*shekel,* and are then reacquired by the wardens so that others might use them as well. Those who seek to fulfill this requirement in the optimal fashion give the half-*shekel* for each member of their family, including minors. If their wives are pregnant, they give the half-*shekel* for the unborn child as well. Once a father has accepted the custom of giving a half-*shekel* for each child, he must continue to do so every year.

The reason why it is customary to give three half-*shekels* is that the Hebrew word *terumah* — contribution — is mentioned three times in the *sidrah* of *Ki Sisa* where the mitzvah of the half-*shekel* is recorded.

The accepted practice is not to view the donation of the half-*shekel* as releasing one from the obligation to give money to the poor on Purim.

THE DAY OF NIKANOR

The thirteenth of Adar is referred to in the Talmud (*Ta'anis* 18b) as "the day of Nikanor." It marks the anniversary of the day when vengeance was exacted during the time of the Chashmonaim. Nikanor was a Greek tyrant who brutally oppressed the Jews in the Land of Israel. He was killed by Yehudah, the son of Mattisyahu, on the thirteenth of Adar and the day was established as a celebration.

THE DAYS OF PURIM

The fourteenth and fifteenth of Adar are celebrated as Purim. The specific day on which Purim is celebrated depends on the locale; in places where Purim is celebrated on the fourteenth, it is not celebrated on the fifteenth and vice versa.

The original observance of Purim as a festival was established by the Sages and the Prophets who decreed that it be observed in every generation. In the *Megillah* we read: TO ESTABLISH THESE DAYS OF PURIM AT THEIR APPROPRIATE TIME (9:31). They explained: AT THEIR APPROPRIATE TIME — i.e., the time appropriate for one [city] is not appropriate for the other [city].

Why were different days established as Purim in different cities? Why wasn't one day chosen as Purim in all cities, just as other festivals are celebrated on the same day in every city?

We find that even in the times of Mordechai and Esther, Purim was celebrated on a different day in Shushan than in the other cities. In all other cities, the battle took place on the thirteenth of Adar and the people rested and celebrated on the fourteenth of Adar. In Shushan however, the battle took place on the thirteenth and fourteenth of Adar. The people only rested and celebrated on the fifteenth of Adar.

By right, only the city of Shushan should celebrate on the fifteenth of Adar, for it was only there that Purim was celebrated on that day. The Sages of that era, however, wanted to accord honor to the Land of Israel which was desolate at the time.

They therefore issued the following ruling: Shushan — where the miracle occurred — has an importance of its own and celebrates Purim on the fifteenth, even though it was not settled and thus did not have a surrounding wall at the time of Yehoshua bin Nun. Other cities which were settled and had walls at the time of Yehoshua bin Nun, even if they are in a state of ruin and are no longer surrounded by walls, are considered to be important. They are therefore accorded the status of Shushan and celebrate Purim on the fifteenth. Cities which did not have surrounding walls at the time of Yehoshua bin Nun — even if they have walls surrounding them today — are to celebrate Purim on the fourteenth of Adar.

The criteria for judging whether a city is given the status of Shushan or not— regarding celebrating Purim on the fifteenth rather than the fourteenth — is thus linked to the state of that city at the time of Yehoshua bin Nun. The present state of the city is not taken into account; i.e., even if the cities in the Land of Israel were desolate at the time that Purim was established, the fact that they were settled and surrounded by walls when Yehoshua bin Nun conquered the Land of Israel gives them an importance which makes them equivalent to Shushan. Their present state of destruction [i.e., at the time when the Sages established Purim] is considered to be temporary.

As regards cities outside the Land of Israel: Even though they may be considered important and may be surrounded by walls today, since they were not important at the time of Yehoshua bin Nun, they are not given the status of Shushan and Purim is celebrated on the fourteenth.

Hence, the Purim which is celebrated on the fourteenth of Adar is referred to as Purim of the "open" [i.e., unimportant or unwalled] cities, whereas the Purim which is celebrated on the fifteenth is referred to as Purim of the "major" [i.e., important or walled] cities.

Today, the only city in which Purim is celebrated on the fifteenth of Adar — besides Shushan — is Jerusalem. Although the *Megillah* is also read on the fifteenth of Adar in a number of other cities in the Land of Israel [e.g., Acco, Yaffo and T'verya], this is only a custom based on the possibility that they may have been surrounded by walls at the time of Yehoshua. We have no means of establishing whether these cities are the same as those which existed at the time of the conquest of the Land of Israel. These cities celebrate Purim on the fourteenth; the additional *Megillah* reading on the fifteenth is a stringency based on doubt as to their status and thus, they do not recite the *berachos* when reading on the fifteenth.

THE OBLIGATIONS OF THE DAY

There are four mitzvos which are obligatory on Purim. These mitzvos were established by the *Sanhedrin* and the Prophets. They are: Reading the *Megillah* of Esther, rejoicing, reciprocal sending of gifts of food and giving gifts to the poor.

The Sages later added other obligations: To read the portion from the *sidrah* of *Beshalach* that tells of the war with Amalek in the desert, and to add the *al ha-nisim* prayer in the *Shemoneh Esreh* and in the Grace after Meals. *Hallel* is not said on Purim. Some maintain that it is unnecessary since the reading of the *Megillah* is itself a form of *Hallel* [praise] to God. Others maintain that we do not recite *Hallel* for a miracle which took place outside the Land of Israel. This second reason is questioned in the Talmud, for it is pointed out that we do say *Hallel* regarding the exodus from Egypt. The Sages answered that until the people entered the Land of Israel, every land was considered to be suitable as regards the recital of *Hallel*. Once they entered the land, however, no other land was considered to be important enough as regards the recital of *Hallel*.

The Talmud offers a third reason as to why we do not recite *Hallel* on Purim. Within *Hallel*, we recite the verse PRAISE HIM SERVANTS OF GOD — i.e., you who are now servants of God, rather than servants of Pharaoh, can offer praise to God. This verse was not applicable, however, to the Jews after the miracle of Purim, for they remained servants of Achashverosh and their exile did not end.

The mitzvos that are obligatory on Purim apply to both "open" and "walled" cities — each on the day on which they celebrate Purim.

♠ Eulogies and fasting are prohibited on both the fourteenth and fifteenth of Adar. Moreover, in a leap year, this prohibition applies to the fourteenth and fifteenth of Adar I as well. One who is in mourning does not observe any of the public signs of mourning on these days — i.e., he does not sit on the ground or remove his shoes. He observes the private aspects of mourning as he would on Shabbos.

✿ Although work is not forbidden on Purim, it is nevertheless considered improper. The Sages said: One who works on Purim will never see any benefit [from that work]. In communities where it is customary to refrain from working on Purim, the religious courts are empowered to punish those who violate the custom.

The work to which we are referring is work undertaken to earn a profit. Work involving the performance of a mitzvah, or work for Purim itself, is always permitted. Additionally, those who celebrate Purim on the fourteenth are allowed to work on the fifteenth and vice versa.

THE THREE DAY PURIM

⚬ When the fifteenth of Adar falls on Shabbos, Purim is celebrated over a three day period in the "walled" cities [Jerusalem and Shushan]. Other cities fulfill all of the obligations of Purim on Friday, the fourteenth. Those who are obligated to celebrate Purim on the fifteenth, however, divide the obligations over the period between the fourteenth and sixteenth. How is this done?

⚬ The mitzvos of reading of the *Megillah* and giving gifts to the poor are fulfilled on the fourteenth of Adar, as in the other cities. On Shabbos, the fifteenth, a second Torah scroll is taken from the *aron kodesh* and the portion from the *sidrah* of *Beshalach* that tells of the war with Amalek is read as the *maftir*. The *al ha-nisim* prayer is added to the *Shemoneh Esreh* and the Grace after Meals. On Sunday, the sixteenth, the mitzvos of the Purim *seudah* [festive meal] and the exchange of

PURIM

gifts of food between friends are fulfilled.

Why was it decided to fulfill the mitzvos of Purim in this manner?

→ Though the *Megillah* should be read in the "walled" cities on the fifteenth, the Sages prohibited the reading of the *Megillah* if this day falls on Shabbos. They feared that the *Megillah* scrolls might be inadvertently carried in the public domain by people who sought someone capable of reading it for them — a violation of the laws of Shabbos. Why then was the reading not delayed until Sunday, the sixteenth? The Sages deduced from the *Megillah* that when the reading cannot be done at the proper time, it should be read earlier than required rather than later. [This is in contradistinction to other Rabbinic obligations — e.g., the fast of *Tishah b'Av* — which are fulfilled later if the time for their fulfillment falls on Shabbos.] The verse in the *Megillah* states: AND THESE DAYS OF PURIM SHALL NOT PASS (*Esther* 9:27) — i.e., we are not permitted to allow the days designated as Purim, the fourteenth and fifteenth of Adar, to pass without our having fulfilled the obligation, but we are permitted to fulfill them earlier than required. Were we to delay the reading of the *Megillah* until Sunday, the sixteenth, we would violate this inferred requirement.

→ The mitzvah of eating the festive Purim *seudah* is delayed until the sixteenth, even though it could theoretically be fulfilled on Shabbos the fifteenth, because of our tradition that we do not mix one celebration [in this case Shabbos] with another [in this case the Purim *seudah*].

→ The giving of gifts to the poor and the exchange of gifts of food between friends cannot be fulfilled on Shabbos, again because we fear that doing so might lead one to inadvertently carry in the public domain. The former obligation is moved to the fourteenth, so that the poor might enjoy their gifts as early as possible. The latter obligation is delayed until the sixteenth

67

since the verse in the *Megillah*, from which we deduced that we do not allow the days of Purim to pass, does not refer to the mitzvah of exchanging gifts. Additionally, by delaying its fulfillment until the sixteenth of Adar, we establish a noticeable difference between the celebration of Purim in the "walled" cities and in other cities.

⚱ Although the mitzvah of reading the *Megillah* can be fulfilled without a *minyan*, when this mitzvah is fulfilled earlier than required [i.e., when the fifteenth falls on Shabbos and the residents of the "walled" cities move the reading to the fourteenth] it is customary to read only in the presence of a *minyan*. This also applies to the reading of the *Megillah* for women; i.e., it should be read in the presence of ten women.

⚱ Additionally, though the exchanging of gifts is delayed until the sixteenth, it is customary for the residents of "walled" cities to also send gifts to friends on the fourteenth. It is also traditional to make the Shabbos meal more elaborate than usual. It is customary for the residents of the walled cities to dress in festive clothing on the sixteenth to indicate that they are celebrating Purim. As noted, the *al ha-nisim* prayer is recited on Shabbos, the fifteenth, and is not recited on the sixteenth — neither in *Shemoneh Esreh* nor in the Grace after Meals.

THE READING OF THE *MEGILLAH*

⚱ One is required to read the *Megillah* both at night and during the day. The obligation at night can be fulfilled from dark until dawn, the obligation to read by day can be fulfilled from sunrise until sunset.

⚱ The mitzvah of reading the *Megillah* applies to both men and women. Optimally, the reading should be done in the presence of a *minyan* in the synagogue. Even if one has a *minyan* in his home, it is still preferable to go to the synagogue for the *Megillah* reading since THE KING'S MAJESTY IS

[MANIFESTED] IN THE MULTITUDES (*Mishlei* 14:28). One of the reasons that we read the *Megillah* is to publicize the miracles of Purim; this is best accomplished when it is read publicly in the synagogues.

&bsp; The reading of the *Megillah* takes precedence over the performance of all positive Torah precepts — even the study of Torah is suspended for the *Megillah* reading. The only mitzvah which we do not suspend for the reading of the *Megillah* is the burial of a person who was found dead and who has no one to provide for his needs.

&bsp; One can fulfill the obligation of reading the *Megillah* by hearing it being read; this is considered tantamount to reading it oneself. The person reading, however, must himself be obligated in this mitzvah [e.g., an adult rather than a minor]. If one is fulfilling the obligation by listening to someone else's reading, he must be careful to hear every word, for if he does not hear the entire *Megillah*, he will not have fulfilled his obligation.

&bsp; It is proper that all those listening to the reading should have a *Megillah* written on parchment in front of them and silently read along. In this manner, one can be certain that even if he failed to hear a word being read, he will have read it by himself and will have thus fulfilled his obligation. If he does not have a *Megillah* written on parchment, he should read along from a printed *Megillah*.

&bsp; The established custom is to spread the *Megillah* out on the reader's table, rather than rolling it as one does with a Torah scroll. The sheets of parchment on which the *Megillah* is written are folded under each other so that the sheets do not hang over the table. The basis for the custom of completely opening the *Megillah* scroll is the verse in Esther which refers to the *Megillah* as a letter. Just as a letter is held completely open when being read, so too should the *Megillah* be completely open when it is read. Additionally, the variation in the method in which we read the *Megillah* serves to publicize the miracle of Purim more widely.

☙ Traditionally, the reader pauses — allowing the congregation to also recite the text — at the four verses in the *Megillah* which speak of Israel's redemption: THERE WAS A JEWISH MAN IN SHUSHAN (*Esther* 2:5), AND MORDECHAI WENT FROM BEFORE THE KING IN ROYAL CLOTHING (ibid. 8:15), THE JEWS HAD ILLUMINATION (ibid. 8:16) and the last verse of the *Megillah*, FOR MORDECHAI WAS DEPUTY TO THE KING (ibid. 10:3). The reader then proceeds to repeat these verses since those who have their obligation fulfilled by listening to the *Megillah* — rather than reading it themselves — must hear every word. The purpose of this custom is to prevent the children from dozing off during the reading. The story of the great miracle performed on Israel's behalf during the time of Mordechai and Esther will thus enter their hearts.

✿ It is also customary for the congregation to read aloud the verse, THAT NIGHT THE SLEEP OF THE KING WAS DISTURBED (ibid. 6:1), and to use a different cantillation for this verse, because this verse marks the point where Israel's salvation began.

✿ The names of Haman's ten sons, the phrase FIVE HUNDRED MEN which precedes them and the word TEN which follows (ibid. 9:6-10) are traditionally read without taking a breath. The purpose of this tradition is to indicate that they were all killed at one time. The inclusion of the phrase FIVE HUNDRED MEN indicates that they were all followers of Haman's sons who served as their commanding officers. If the reader failed to read these passages without taking a breath, one has still fulfilled the mitzvah.

THE *BERACHOS* RECITED ON THE *MEGILLAH*

☙ The person reading the *Megillah* recites three *berachos* before beginning and one *berachah* after completing the reading. He must have conscious intent to discharge the obligation of those listening to him. The congregation should answer *amen* to his *berachos* and have conscious intent to have their obligation discharged through him. The refrain *baruch hu u'varuch shemo* — usually said when hearing the first phrase of a *berachah* — is not said when the reader recites the *berachos* on the *Megillah* so as not to interrupt the *berachah*. The three *berachos* recited before the reading are:

Blessed are You...who has sanctified us with His mitzvos and has commanded us concerning the reading of the *Megillah*.

Blessed are You...who performed miracles for our fathers, in those days at this time.

Blessed are You ... who has kept us alive, and sustained us and enabled us to reach this time.

🔊 After the *Megillah* reading, the following *berachah* is recited:

Blessed are You...who fights our battles, and judges our cases ...

🔊 This *berachah* is followed by two paragraphs, as found in the *Siddur*. The second paragraph, *Shoshanas Yaakov*, contains a reference to Haman being cursed and Mordechai being blessed. This is in fulfillment of the Talmud's dictum that one is required to curse Haman and bless Mordechai on Purim. After the *Megillah* reading in the morning, the first paragraph, *Asher Heini*, is not said.

🔊 The three *berachos* recited at night are repeated before the *Megillah* reading during the day. However, when the reader recites the *shehecheyanu* — the third *berachah* — during the day, he should have intent that the *berachah* apply to the other mitzvos of Purim as well; i.e., gifts to the poor, exchanging gifts of food with friends and the festive Purim meal. Some communities have a custom of not reciting *shehecheyanu* during the day. They therefore have intent that the *berachah* recited before the *Megillah* reading at night apply to the special *mitzvos* of Purim which are fulfilled during the day.

♫ If one reads the *Megillah* alone, only the *berachos* before the reading are recited. The *berachah* that follows is omitted. If one had already fulfilled his obligation vis-a-vis the *Megillah* reading, and he wished to read it again publicly for others, he recites the *berachos* before and after the reading. If one reads the *Megillah* for an individual, the *berachah* after the reading is omitted. If the person listening is capable, it is preferable that he recite the *berachos*.

✿ It is customary to roll the *Megillah* back into a scroll before reciting the *berachah* after the reading, for it is considered disrespectful to leave the *Megillah* open.

♫ When the *Megillah* is read for women, the text of the first *berachah* is changed because women are only obligated to hear the *Megillah* but not to read it. They therefore recite *to hear the Megillah* rather than *to read the Megillah*. In Sefardic communities, the *berachos* are not recited when the *Megillah* is read for women.

♫ If a person who lives in a city where the *Megillah* is read on the fourteenth of Adar travels to a city where the *Megillah* is read on the fifteenth [e.g., to Jerusalem] or vice-versa, there are many variables that must be taken into account so as to determine when he is required to hear the *Megillah* reading. The halachah itself is disputed by different authorities. It is therefore advisable when one leaves his home on the thirteenth of Adar without intending to return on the same day to consult with a halachic authority as to the proper time to hear the reading of the *Megillah* as well as to fulfill the other obligations of the day.

EXCERPTS FROM THE COMMENTARIES TO THE *MEGILLAH*

Not all of Israel participated in the feast arranged by Achashverosh. The verse states: AND HE MADE A FEAST FOR ALL OF THE PEOPLE WHO WERE IN SHUSHAN (*Esther* 1:3). R. Chama bar

Chanina explained: This indicates that only the common people participated in the feast — the elders of the community heard about the feast and fled. R. Shimon bar Yochai said: This indicates that they were forced to eat foods prepared by non-Jews, who would say to Israel, "Is your God capable of preparing a feast as lavish as this in the World to Come?" They [the Jews] responded: NO EYE HAS SEEN BESIDES YOU, GOD, WHAT SHALL BE DONE FOR THOSE WHO AWAIT YOU (Yeshayahu 64:3). If He prepares a feast such as this, we shall say: 'We have already eaten a feast such as this in the presence of Achashverosh.'"

AND HE [ACHASHVEROSH] PLACED HIS [HAMAN'S] CHAIR ABOVE THE OTHER MINISTERS (Esther 3:1) — to what can this be compared? There was once a man who had a horse, a donkey and a pig. He would carefully measure the food which he gave the donkey and the horse, but he allowed the pig to eat as much as he wanted. One day, the horse said to the donkey: "We, who serve our master, receive food that is measured out carefully, while the pig, who does nothing at all, receives as much food as he wants." The donkey replied to the horse: "Wait and see what happens." When the holiday of the people arrived, they took the pig and slaughtered him. In the same vein, the verse tells us: AND THE KING ELEVATED HAMAN IN STATURE (ibid.).

AND HAMAN SOUGHT TO ANNIHILATE ALL OF THE JEWS (ibid. 3:6) — to what can this be compared? There was once a bird who built his nest at the seashore, but the tides came and washed his nest away. What did he do? He began to fill his beak with water and then spit the water onto the sand, repeating this action over and over. A friend of his came and saw what he was doing.

"To what end do you exert yourself?" he asked.

He answered: "I will not move from here until I make the sea into sand and the sand into sea!"

In the same vein, God told Haman: "Wicked one, you seek to annihilate all the Jews! I sought to do so and was unable, as the verse states, HE SAID THEY WOULD BE DESTROYED [AND THEY WOULD HAVE BEEN] HAD MOSHE HIS CHOSEN NOT STOOD IN THE BREACH (Tehillim 106:23). And you [Haman] imagine that you shall be able to do so!"

Rava said: There was no one who knew how to slander as well as Haman. [He told Achashverosh,] THERE IS ONE NATION WHO IS SCATTERED IN EVERY PROVINCE OF YOUR KINGDOM, AND THEIR BELIEFS ARE DIFFERENT FROM THOSE OF ANY OTHER PEOPLE, AND THEY DO NOT FULFILL THE LAWS OF THE KING AND IT IS NOT WORTH THE KING'S WHILE TO ALLOW THEM TO REMAIN (Esther 3:8).

Haman said to Achashverosh: "Come, let us annihilate the Jews."

Achashverosh replied: "I am afraid of their God, for He may do to me what He did to my predecessor."

Haman answered: "They are asleep [the spelling of yashnu — they are asleep — is identical to yeshno — there is — the first word in Haman's proposal to the king] in their performance of the mitzvos, and they lack a source of merit through which their God might save them."

Achashverosh told Haman: "But there are among them rabbis and pious men who have not sinned [and they will provide merit]!"

Haman replied: "They are one nation, and the pious among them are as guilty as the wicked." Haman continued: "Do not fear that by annihilating the Jews I shall make one of your provinces lack population, for the Jews are scattered and their slaughter will make no noticeable impression. If you think that they live alone in some small city which it would be a pity to render desolate, know that the Jews are to be found IN EVERY PROVINCE IN YOUR KINGDOM (ibid.) .

THEIR BELIEFS ARE DIFFERENT FROM THOSE OF ANY OTHER PEOPLE — Haman went on. "They will not eat what we cook, they do not take our daughters for their sons nor will they give their daughters to our sons. AND THEY DO NOT FULFILL THE LAWS OF THE KING — Throughout the year they avoid doing the king's bidding, claiming: 'Today is Shabbos, today is Pesach and we are forbidden to work.' IT IS NOT WORTH THE KING'S WHILE TO ALLOW THEM TO REMAIN — Even when they eat and drink, they deride the king. If a fly falls into one of their cups, they throw out the fly and continue drinking the wine. But if my master, the king, were to touch a cup belonging to one of them, he would pour the wine onto the ground and not drink it" (*Megillah* 13a-b).

TEN THOUSAND KIKAR OF SILVER — Why was Haman willing to give ten thousand *kikar* of silver to destroy the Jews? Haman said: "The entire merit of the Jews is the fact that they each donated a half-*shekel* towards the support of the *Mishkan* [Tabernacle]. I will give an amount equivalent to all of the half-*shekels* that the 600,000 Jews donated throughout their lives. The obligation to donate the half-*shekel* is incumbent only upon males who have reached the age of twenty. The normal lifespan of a man is until the age of seventy. The amount that they all gave in those fifty years comes to exactly ten thousand *kikar* of silver. Let my *shekalim* come and annul the power of theirs" (*Chizkuni* to *Parashas Ki Sisa*).

Resh Lakish said: It was known and clear to He who spoke and the world came about that Haman would weigh out *shekalim*

so as to annihilate Israel. God therefore ordered that their [i.e., Israel's] *shekalim* be given before his [Haman's]. It is for this reason that it was ordained that on the first day of Adar, we announce the requirement to donate the *shekalim*.

AND ESTHER SAID TO REPLY TO MORDECHAI: FAST FOR ME — DO NOT EAT AND DO NOT DRINK FOR THREE DAYS (*Esther* 4:16). The three days were the thirteenth, fourteenth and fifteenth of Nisan. Mordechai replied to her: "Among them [i.e., the days that you ask us to fast for you] is the first day of Pesach [when we are not permitted to fast]!" She answered him: "Elder of Israel, of what purpose is Pesach [if Israel is annihilated]!" Mordechai heard her response and admitted that she was right (*Esther Rabbah*).

The Sages taught: Why did Esther invite Haman to join with her in the feast that she had prepared for Achashverosh?

R. Eliezer explained: She prepared a trap for him, as the verse states: LET THEIR TABLES BE A TRAP IN FRONT OF THEM (*Tehillim* 69:23).

R. Yehoshua said: She learned this from her father, as the verse states: IF YOUR ENEMY IS HUNGRY, FEED HIM BREAD. IF HE IS THIRSTY, GIVE HIM WATER TO DRINK, FOR BY DOING SO, YOU HEAP BURNING EMBERS UPON HIS HEAD (*Mishlei* 25:21-22).

R. Meir said: She wanted to insure that he [Haman] did not plot to overthrow the king, for the time was propitious for Haman.

R. Yehudah said: She wanted to insure that no one learn that she was a Jewess.

R. Nechemyah said: She wanted to insure that the Jews did not become overconfident and say, "We have a sister in the royal household," and thereby refrain from seeking Divine mercy.

R. Yosi said: She wanted him to be in her presence at all times so that she might find a means to trap him into some misdeed in the king's presence.

R. Shimon ben Menasya said: [Esther thought that] God, seeing that she too was forced to curry favor with Israel's enemy, to flatter him and lessen her own honor, would perform a miracle for the Jews.

R. Yehoshua ben Karcha said: [Esther said to herself,] "I will show him friendship so that the king might become jealous and kill us both."

Rabban Gamliel said: He [Achashverosh] was an unstable king and would go back on his word. She said to herself, "Perhaps I shall be able to entrap him [Haman] and he will be killed. And if the opportunity does not present itself, perhaps he [Achashverosh] will change his mind."

Rabban Gamliel added: We still need [the explanation of R. Eliezer] ha-Modai [to understand Esther's motivation]. We learned — R. Eliezer ha-Modai explained: She caused the king to be jealous [by inviting Haman] and she caused the other ministers to be jealous [by inviting Haman alone].

Raba said: [Esther acted in accordance with the verse that states:] BEFORE THE DOWNFALL THERE IS PRIDE (Mishlei 16:18).

Abbaye and Rava both explained: [Esther acted in accordance with the verse that states:] IN THEIR HEAT [OF ANGER] I WILL SET THEIR DRINKS AND I WILL MAKE THEM INTOXICATED SO THAT THEY MIGHT EXULT. AND THEY WILL FALL INTO AN ETERNAL SLEEP AND WILL NOT AWAKEN (Yirmeyahu 51:39). [The verse refers specifically to Belshatzar. Esther took this as proof that when the wicked drink, calamity befalls them.]

Raba bar Avahu met Eliyahu and asked him: "According to whose opinion did Esther act?" Eliyahu replied: "In accordance with the opinion of all of the tannaim and amoraim."

HAMAN'S LETTER TO THE NATIONS — WRITTEN IN THE NAME
OF ACHASHVEROSH

Endless peace be unto you.

Let it be known to you that there is one man among us who is
not from this locale, but who comes from royal stock — from
the seed of Amalek. He is among the greatest of the generation
and his name is Haman.

He has made a small request of us regarding one nation that
resides among us — a contemptible people who are arrogant,
seek our harm and who curse the king. And how do they curse
us? They say: GOD REIGNS FOREVER; THE NATIONS SHALL BE
BANISHED FROM HIS LAND (Tehillim 10:16). They also say: TO TAKE
VENGEANCE FROM THE NATIONS, REPROOF FROM THE
NATIONALITIES (ibid. 149:7). They acknowledge no gratitude to
those who have bestowed good upon them.

Come and see what they did to poor Pharaoh. When they went
down to Egypt, he welcomed them cordially and settled them in
the best part of his land. He fed them in the years of famine —
giving them the very best produce of the land. He sought to
build a palace for himself and he had them do the building.
Despite all that he did for them, he could not prevail against
them. Moreover, they came to him with excuses and said: "WE
SHALL GO FOR A TRIP OF THREE DAYS TO OFFER SACRIFICES TO OUR
GOD (Shemos 3:18). Afterwards, we shall return — lend us silver
and gold vessels and clothing." The Egyptians lent them silver
and gold and their finest clothing. Each of them loaded mules
without end until they had emptied the land of Egypt — and
then they fled!

When Pharaoh learned that they had run away, he went after
them so as to return his belongings. And what did they do to
him? Among them was a man named Moshe, the son of
Amram, who was a great magician. He took his magic staff and

whispered an incantation and then struck the sea until it became dry. This entire people then entered the dried out sea and passed through. I do not know how they passed through or how the sea became dry.

When Pharaoh saw what was happening, he followed them so as to return his belongings. I do not know how they pushed him into the sea, but he and his armies were drowned there! They did not show any gratitude for all of the good that he had done for them — you can see that they are ingrates!

Furthermore, see what they did to Amalek, my grandfather, when he attacked them. AND AMALEK CAME AND FOUGHT WITH ISRAEL AT REFIDIM. From where did Amalek come? R. Kruspedai said in the name of R. Yochanan: Amalek came from Bil'am, whom he had approached for advice. Amalek told Bil'am: "We know that you give advice and that you are a master of evil thoughts. Anyone who takes your advice is assured that he will not fail. You see what this people have done to the Egyptians who were good to them. Imagine what they shall do to the other nations! What advice can you offer us?" Bil'am told him: "Go and wage war with them, for if you do battle with them, you shall succeed. Their merit is based on the fact that they are descendants of Avraham. Since you too are a descendant of Avraham, you can also rely on his merit."

Immediately, they [Amalek] attacked them. What did Moshe, their leader, do? He had a disciple named Yehoshua bin Nun — a cruel and merciless man. Moshe told him: "Choose men for us and go and wage war with Amalek." I do not know if the men that he chose were magicians or heroes. What did Moshe then do? He took his staff in his hand — I do not know how he used it. When they came upon Amalek, I do not know what incantation he whispered. But they [Amalek] were weakened, and fell before the Jews.

When they came upon Sichon and Og — the mightiest warriors

of our land before whom no one could stand — they killed them though I do not know how. The kings of Midian attacked them and I do not know how they killed them.

What else did this disciple of the man Moshe do? He brought them into the land of Canaan. It was not enough that he stole their land — he killed thirty-one kings and parcelled out the land to Israel without mercy. Those who he did not kill became his servants.

When Sisro attacked with his armies, I do not know what they [Israel] did. The Kishon stream gathered them [Sisro's armies] and cast them into the sea.

Their first king — his name was Shaul — waged war in the land of my grandfather, Amalek, and slaughtered a hundred thousand riders in one day! He had no mercy; slaughtering men, women, children — I do not know how he did this! And what they did to Agag — my grandfather — to whom they had at first shown mercy! A man named Shemuel came and cut his flesh into strips and fed it to the birds! I do not know how he killed him.

Later, they had a king named David, the son of Yishai. He destroyed all of the kingdoms in the area without mercy. He was followed by his son Shelomo, who built a house for Israel which he called the Beis ha-Mikdash. I do not know what they had inside that house. When they would prepare to wage war, they would enter that house and practice sorcery, and when they emerged they would slaughter and destroy the world.

Because of the abundance of good which they enjoyed, they rebelled against their God. Moreover, their God has grown old. Nevuchadnezer came, burned their house and exiled them from their land, settling them in our midst. They still have not changed their repulsive beliefs. Although they're exiled among us, they ridicule us and the faith that we place in our gods.

Now, we have all reached agreement. We have cast lots to determine the appropriate time to annihilate them. The lot fell on the thirteenth day of the month of Adar. When this letter reaches you, prepare yourselves on that date to slaughter and totally destroy all of the Jews who dwell among you — young and old, children and women — and do not allow a remnant of them to survive (*Esther Rabbah*).

HAMAN AND THE SCHOOLCHILDREN

When the letters were sealed and given to Haman, he and his allies were overjoyed. They met Mordechai who was walking along. Mordechai saw three children coming from school and ran after them. When Haman and his friends saw Mordechai running after the schoolchildren, they followed him to find out what it was that Mordechai sought from the children. When Mordechai caught up to the children, he asked one of them: "Tell me the verse that you studied today." The child replied: HAVE NO FEAR OF SUDDEN DREAD OR OF THE CALAMITY OF THE WICKED WHEN IT COMES (*Mishlei* 3:25). The second child responded: "It was my turn to read today, and this is the verse that I learned. [THEY TAKE COUNSEL] AND IT SHALL BE NULLIFIED, SPEAK A WORD AND IT DOES NOT TRANSPIRE, FOR GOD IS WITH US (*Yeshayahu* 8:10). The third child answered: UNTIL OLD AGE I AM, AND UNTIL RIPE AGE I SHALL BEAR. I HAVE DONE AND I SHALL BEAR — I SHALL ENDURE AND I SHALL SAVE (ibid. 46:4).

When Mordechai heard the verses which they had quoted, he began to laugh and became happy. Haman asked him: "What is it that these children said that has made you so happy?"

Mordechai answered: "The good news that they have brought me — that I need have no fear of the evil counsel which you have contrived!"

Haman, the wicked, became very angry and said: "I shall start the slaughter with these children!" (*Esther Rabbah* 7).

THREE VERSES — THREE WARS

Why did Mordechai rejoice when he heard the children quote these three verses? These verses allude to the three wars that Amalek fought with Israel. Their content showed that Haman's plot against Israel would be foiled just as the earlier plans of Amalek had come to naught.

The first time that Amalek waged war against Israel, they had attacked the Jews suddenly, as the verse states: AND THEY HAPPENED UPON YOU WHILE YOU WERE ON YOUR WAY (*Devarim* 25:18). The first verse quoted applies to this war, for it states: HAVE NO FEAR OF SUDDEN DREAD (*Mishlei* 3:25).

The second time that Amalek fought with Israel, they came disguised as Canaanites in order to confuse Israel so that they might not recognize them and therefore not know how to pray. The verse states: AND THE CANAANITES [I.E., AMALEK WHO DISGUISED THEMSELVES AS CANAANITES] HEARD...AND THEY WAGED WAR WITH ISRAEL (*Bemidbar* 21:1). The second verse applied to this war — TAKE COUNSEL AND IT SHALL BE NULLIFIED (*Yeshayahu* 8:10).

The third time that Amalek came was now, when Haman imagined that he would be successful, claiming that God had grown old and was no longer capable of saving His house from destruction by Nevuchadnezer, or His people [see Haman's letter to the nations]. The third verse applied to this war — UNTIL OLD AGE I AM (ibid. 46:4). (Gra)

THE CALL OF THE SHEEP

When Haman completed the construction of the scaffold, he

went to Mordechai and found him in the study hall, the children gathered around him in sackcloth, studying Torah and crying. Haman counted them and found that there were twenty-two thousand children. He had them chained and sent guards to watch them, declaring: "Tomorrow, I will slaughter these children and then I will hang Mordechai."

Their mothers brought them bread and water and told them: "Children, eat and drink before you are killed so that you might not die first of hunger."

The children placed their hands on their books and swore: "By the life of our teacher, Mordechai! We shall neither eat nor drink, but shall die while fasting."

They began to weep until their tears of anguish ascended to the heavens. God heard their crying...and at that time, His mercy became aroused, and He rose from His seat of judgement and sat on His seat of mercy.

God said: "What is this loud sound that I hear which is like the bleating of kids and sheep?"

Moshe *Rabbenu* stood up before God and said: "Master of the Universe, these are not kids or sheep, but rather, the little ones of Your people who have been fasting for three days and three nights. Tomorrow, the enemy seeks to slaughter them like kids and sheep."

At this point, God took the decrees which He had issued concerning them, and which had been sealed with a seal of clay. He ripped them and caused Achashverosh to become confused, as the verse states: THAT NIGHT THE SLEEP OF THE KING WAS DISTURBED (Esther 6:1). (Esther Rabbah 9)

MORDECHAI'S PRAYER

Mordechai prayed to God and said: "It is known and clear before

83

the throne of Your glory, Master of the Universe, that the reason I refused to bow down to Haman was not because of my arrogance and pride. Rather, I acted as I did because of my awe for You, for I fear You and would not give the honor due You to flesh and blood. I did not want to prostrate myself to anyone but You. Whom am I to refuse to bow to Haman so as to save Your people, Israel?

"And, You, God — save us please from his [Haman's] hand, and may he sink into the abyss which he has dug. May he be ensnared in the trap which he has prepared for Your pious ones. Let this agitator realize that You have not forgotten the promise that You have made to us: AND EVEN THIS; WHEN THEY ARE IN THE LAND OF THEIR ENEMIES I WILL NOT REJECT THEM NOR WILL I FIND THEM DESPICABLE AND THEREBY DESTROY THEM THUS VIOLATING MY COVENANT WITH THEM, FOR I AM THE LORD THEIR GOD (*Vayikra* 26:44).

What did Mordechai then do? He gathered the children, withheld bread and water from them, dressed them in sackcloth and sat them in the dust. And they cried and wept and occupied themselves with the Torah. (*Esther Rabbah* 8)

ESTHER'S PRAYER

At this time, Esther was very frightened by the danger which Israel faced. She removed her royal garments and dressed in sackcloth. She uncovered her hair and spread ashes and dust. She afflicted herself by fasting and prostrated herself before God and began to pray.

"God, Lord of Israel, who has ruled since the beginning of days and who created the world. Help Your maidservant who is orphaned of father and mother, and who is like a poor person who goes to beg from door to door. I too seek Your mercy as I go from window to window in the house of Achashverosh. And now, God, grant success to Your impoverished maidservant, and save the flock which You tend from the enemies who rise up against us. There is nothing to restrain You from saving us — the many or the few. And You, father of orphans, stand by the side of this poor orphan who trusts in Your grace, that she might find favor in the eyes of this man, for I fear him. Cast him down before me, for You cast down the haughty." (*Esther Rabbah* 8)

ESTHER ENTERS THE INNER COURTYARD

On the third day [of the fast — the fifteenth of Nisan], Esther put on her finest clothing and most precious jewelry. Accompanied by two of her maidservants, she placed her right hand on one to lean on her as befits a queen, while the second maidservant followed her mistress and held her adornments so that they not touch the ground. Her face was radiant and she hid her anxiety. She entered the inner courtyard and stood opposite the king.

The king was seated on his throne, clothed in gold and precious jewels. He looked up and saw Esther standing before him, and he became angry, for she had violated his decree and had come to him without being called.

Esther looked up and saw the king's face — his eyes were afire because of the anger that burned inside him. When she saw his anger, Esther became frightened and faint, and she placed her head on the shoulder of the maidservant who stood on her right.

But our God saw and He was filled with mercy for His people, and He paid heed to the anguish of the poor orphan who had placed her trust in Him. He granted her favor in the eyes of the king and He increased her beauty and the majesty of her presence.

The king arose from his throne in confusion. He ran to Esther and embraced her and kissed her. He placed his arm around her neck and said: "Queen Esther, why do you fear? The rule which we have established does not apply to you, for you are my beloved companion. Why," he continued, "did you not speak to me when I noticed you?"

Esther replied: "My master, the king, when I saw you I became nervous because of your majesty."

The king then said: "WHAT IS YOUR WISH, QUEEN ESTHER, AND WHAT IS YOUR REQUEST?" (*Esther* 5:3).

Esther answered: "IF IT MEETS THE KING'S FAVOR, LET THE KING AND HAMAN COME TO THE FEAST..." (ibid. 5:4). (*Esther Rabbah 9*)

ZERESH'S ADVICE

AND WHEN HAMAN SAW MORDECHAI SITTING AT THE ENTRANCE TO THE KING'S PALACE AND HE DID NOT RISE OR MOVE BEFORE HIM, HAMAN BECAME FILLED WITH ANGER. AND HAMAN RESTRAINED HIMSELF... AND HE BROUGHT HIS LOVED ONES AND ZERESH HIS WIFE (*Esther* 5:9-10).

Haman had 365 advisors — one for each day of the year. None of them could offer advice that was as efficacious as that offered by Zeresh.

She told him: "This man [Mordechai] about whom you seek advice: If he is of the seed of the Jews, you will not prevail against him. Your only hope is to employ a tactic which none of his people have ever experienced. Should you try to kill him by casting him into a furnace — Chananyah and his companions have already been saved from this. If you throw him into a lion's den — Daniel has already come out of one alive. If you imprison him — Yosef has already emerged from one. If you lock him into an iron box and light a fire underneath it —

Menasheh once prayed and God answered him and he survived. If you exile him into the desert — his [Mordechai's] ancestors already were fruitful and multiplied while sojourning in the desert. They faced numerous trials, but they withstood them all and were saved. If you blind him — Shimshon killed many Phillistines even though he was blind. Rather, hang him on a scaffold, for we have never seen any of his nation saved from this type of death. Immediately, THE IDEA FOUND FAVOR BEFORE HAMAN AND HE MADE THE SCAFFOLD (ibid.).

HAMAN'S SCAFFOLD

From which type of wood was Haman's scaffold made? The Sages said: When Haman started its construction, God called together all of the trees that had been created and said, "Who will volunteer that this wicked man be hung upon them?"

The fig tree said: "I will volunteer, for Israel brings their *bikkurim* from my fruit and they are themselves compared to a fig tree."

The vine said: "I will volunteer, for Israel is compared to me."

The pomegranate said: "I will volunteer, for Israel is compared to me."

The nut tree said: I will volunteer, for Israel is compared to me."

The *esrog* said: "I will volunteer, for Israel uses me to fulfill a mitzvah."

The myrtle said: "I will volunteer, for Israel is compared to me."

The olive, the apple and the palm tree all said: "We will volunteer, for Israel is compared to us."

The acacia and the cypress said: "We will volunteer, for we are compared to *tzaddikim*."

The willow said: "I will volunteer, for I am used to fulfill the mitzvah of the four species."

The thorn then said to God: "Master of the Universe, I who have no merit on which to base my claim — I volunteer that this defiled one [Haman] be hung upon me. I am called a thorn and he is a painful thorn, and it is fitting that the thorn be hung upon the thorn." And the tree which they [Haman's friends] found was a thorn and from it they made the scaffold.

When the scaffold was brought to his [Haman's] home, they set it up and he demonstrated how he intended to hang Mordechai from it. A Divine voice then said: "The scaffold is fitting for you — it has been waiting for you since the six days of creation!" (*Esther Rabbah* 9).

THE KING'S SLEEP WAS DISTURBED

THAT NIGHT THE KING'S SLEEP WAS DISTURBED (*Esther* 6:1) — R. Tanchum said: This refers to the sleep of the King of the Universe. Does the Omnipresent sleep? Does the verse not state: BEHOLD THE GUARDIAN OF ISAEL NEITHER DOZES NOR SLEEPS (*Tehillim* 121:4). When Israel is troubled and the nations of the world are serene [it appears as if God is asleep] as the verse states: AWAKEN! WHY DO YOU SLEEP GOD? (ibid. 44:24)

The Sages explained: Those above were disturbed and those below were disturbed. Those above were disturbed — so as to awaken mercy. Those below were disturbed — R. Chami bar Chanina said: None who were capable of sleep, slept that night. Esther was busy preparing the feast for Haman. Mordechai was occupied with his sackcloth and his fast. Haman was occupied with his scaffold. At this time, God told the angel who is in charge of sleep: "My children are in trouble and this wicked one

[Achashverosh] sleeps on his bed! Go and disturb his sleep." The angel immediately descended, stood by Achashverosh's bed and beat him on his heart, saying: "Ingrate! Go and repay the one to whom [the reward for having saved the king's life — i.e., Mordechai] is due."

Rava explained: The reference is to Achashverosh's sleep. He began to think to himself: "What is the meaning of Esther's invitation to Haman? Perhaps they are plotting to assassinate me!" Achashverosh then told himself: "If it is true that they are conspiring against me, is it possible that I do not have a single friend who would warn me?" He then thought: "Perhaps there is someone who did me a favor and I have not yet rewarded him! Perhaps this is the reason why people are reluctant to tell me what is going on. Immediately, HE [ACHASHVEROSH] TOLD THEM [HIS SERVANTS] TO BRING THE BOOK OF REMEMBRANCE (ibid. 6:1).

R. Levi said: Haman's son was the king's scribe and read what was written in the royal chronicles. [He read to Achashverosh from the chronicles, but when he reached the entry] which states, AND IT WAS DISCOVERED THAT WHICH MORDECHAI HAD RELATED ABOUT BIGSAN AND SERESH, he began to roll the scroll.

The king told him: "How long will you go on rolling the scroll? Read what is written!"

He [Haman's son] responded: "I cannot read."

The verses began to read themselves and Achashverosh heard the words, THAT WHICH MORDECHAI HAD RELATED... When he heard Mordechai's name mentioned, he [the king] fell back asleep (Megillah 15; Esther Rabbah 10; Yalkut Shimoni to Esther 1057).

ACHASHVEROSH'S DREAM AND ITS INTERPRETATION

Towards morning, the king had a dream. He saw Haman standing over him with his sword unsheathed. Haman was removing the king's royal garments and crown and was preparing to kill him. At that very moment, Haman himself came and knocked at the king's door. The king awoke startled and asked: "Who is in the courtyard?"

His servants told him: "Haman is standing in the courtyard."

Achashverosh thought to himself, "I have not been dreaming." He then told his servants: "Let him enter."

When he entered, the king said to him: "What should be done for a man whom the king desires to honor?"

Haman started to swell with pride, thinking: "Who is greater than I am? Who is more deserving of honor than I am? Whatever I suggest will be done for me!" He then said: "My master, the king. For a man whom the king desires to honor — let them bring the royal garments...and the steed...and the royal crown."

When Haman mentioned the royal crown, the king's expression changed and he said to himself: "This is what I saw in my dream. He wants to kill me!" He said to Haman: "Quickly, take the garments and steed and do as you have suggested to Mordechai!"

Haman asked: "My master, the king. There are many Mordechais in this world?"

The king answered: "I refer to Mordechai the Jew."

Haman asked: "But there are many Mordechais among the Jews?"

The king answered: "The one who sits at the entrance to the king's palace."

Haman asked: "If this is the one whom you desire to honor, it is sufficient to give him one village or one stream."

The king began to roar like a lion and told him: "Do not leave out one detail of that which you have suggested!"

The king then called for Hasach and Charvonah and ordered them to accompany Haman. He instructed them: "Be careful that he not omit a single detail of that which he suggested." The two of them then went with Haman (*Pesikta Rabbah* 18).

Haman went to the king's royal storage house, bent over with his head hanging as if he was in mourning. His eyes were dark, his mouth contorted, his heart pounding and his knees shaking. He took the king's robes and vestments, and quickly proceeded to the royal stables. There, he selected the finest horse on which a gold chain hung. Taking hold of the reins, he carried the royal clothing on his shoulder and went to Mordechai's home.

When Mordechai saw Haman approaching with the horse, he said to himself: "It seems to me that this wicked man is only coming so as to have me trampled by his horse." Mordechai's disciples were sitting and studying in front of him. He told them: "Stand up and flee so that you might not be burned by my embers."

They replied: "We shall not leave you — in life or in death we shall stay with you!"

Mordechai immediately put on his *tallis* and began to pray. In the meantime, Haman entered and sat down among the students.

He asked them: "What are you studying?"

They replied: "The laws of the *omer*, which Israel offered when the *Beis ha-Mikdash* stood." [Haman came to Mordechai on the sixteenth of Nisan — the day on which the *omer* was offered. Thus, the material that Mordechai had been studying with the students was relevant to that date.]

Haman asked them: "And this *omer* offering — was it brought from gold or silver?"

"It was brought from barley," they replied.

"And how much was it worth?" he asked.

"A great deal," they answered. "Ten *maos*."

Haman said: "Your ten *maos* have prevailed over my ten thousand *kikar* of silver!"

When Mordechai finished praying, Haman addressed him: "Arise, Mordechai the righteous, son of Avraham, Yitzchak and Yaakov. Your sackcloth and ashes have prevailed over my ten thousand *kikar* of silver. Remove your sackcloth and ashes and dress in the king's clothing and mount the king's steed."

Mordechai replied: "Wicked one, son of the descendant of Amalek! Wait an hour until I have eaten bitter bread and drank bitter water. Then you can take me out and hang me on the scaffold."

Haman told him: "Arise, Mordechai the righteous. For as long as you have lived, great miracles have been performed for you. The scaffold which I have prepared is to my detriment. Now rise and put on the royal cloak, place the crown on your head and mount the steed, for the king wishes to pay you honor."

Mordechai understood that God had performed a miracle for him. He turned to Haman and said: "Fool, this is not fitting! I sit in sackcloth and ashes and my body is grimy. Can I wear royal vestments? I will not put on these clothes until I have bathed and have had my hair trimmed."

Haman went to search for a bath attendant and a barber, but could find none. Haman therefore took Mordechai to the bath house and attended him, bringing him all sorts of perfumes and lotions, washing him and rubbing him with oil. He also brought scissors from his home and trimmed his hair. While shaving him, Haman began to sigh.

"Why do you sigh?" Mordechai asked.

Haman replied: "Woe to the man who was the greatest among the nobles and whose throne was above all the others — he has become a bath attendant and a barber!"

Mordechai responded: "Wicked one! Do I not remember your father who was a bath attendant and a barber for twenty-two years in Kfar Krinus? Are these not his instruments?"

When Haman had finished dressing Mordechai, he told him: "Mount and ride the horse."

Mordechai replied: "I am old and weak from my fast."

Haman bent down and lowered his neck. Mordechai stepped on Haman and mounted the horse, kicking him as he did so.

"Mordechai, does the verse not say, WHEN YOUR ENEMY FALLS DO NOT REJOICE?" (Mishlei 24:17).

Mordechai answered: "Wicked one, the verse also states, AND YOU SHALL TREAD ON THEIR HEIGHTS!" (Devarim 33:29) .

Mordechai rode while Haman walked in front of him announcing: "Thus is done to the man whom the king desires to honor." Twenty-seven thousand courtiers, with gold cups in their right hands and silver cups in their left hands, also paraded and declared: "Thus is done to the man whom the king desires to honor." All in attendance praised Mordechai and held lit torches. Haman's daughter looked out the window; when she saw her father's embarrassment, she fell and died.

When the Jews saw the honor being paid to Mordechai, they paraded on either side of him and said: "Thus is done to the man whom the King in heaven desires to honor."

Mordechai also sang praise and said: I WILL MAKE YOU EXALTED GOD, FOR YOU HAVE SAVED ME AND YOU HAVE NOT ALLOWED MY ENEMIES TO REJOICE (*Tehillim* 30:2).

Mordechai's disciples said: SING TO GOD YOU WHO ARE HIS FOLLOWERS. GIVE THANKS TO HIS HOLY NAME, FOR HIS ANGER IS MOMENTARY AND LIFE IS DEPENDENT UPON HIS WILL (ibid. 30:5-6).

Esther said: TO YOU, GOD, I CALLED AND TO YOU, GOD, I PLEADED. WHAT PROFIT IS THERE IN MY BLOOD? (ibid. 30:9-10).

The Jews said: YOU HAVE TRANSFORMED MY MOURNING INTO DANCING FOR ME (ibid. 30:12).

HAMAN STAGGERED BACK TO HIS HOME (*Esther* 6:12) trained in four professions — bath attendant, barber, orderly and announcer! (*Megillah* 16a-b; *Esther Rabbah* 10; *Vayikra Rabbah* 28).

AND MORDECHAI WOULD NOT KNEEL NOR BOW (*Esther* 3:2) — Why did Mordechai endanger Israel by enraging Haman? The Sages explained: Haman placed an idol on his chest, so as to force Israel to violate the transgression of idolatry when they would bow down to him. Idolatry is one of the three sins for which a Jew is required to give up his life rather than transgress — hence, Mordechai refused to bow down.

The verse states, AND MORDECHAI WOULD NOT KNEEL NOR BOW, using the future form rather than the past form, AND MORDE-CHAI DID NOT KNEEL NOR BOW. This indicates that Mordechai made it clear to Haman that he would never kneel or bow. Although Mordechai could have avoided Haman, he chose not to do so. Rather, he intentionally sought him out to demonstrate his refusal, for Mordechai was a descendant of Binyamin.

When Yaakov had prostrated himself in front of Esav, Binyamin had not yet been born. Consequently, Binyamin's descendants had never become accustomed to subjugating themselves to the descendants of Esav.

Some commentaries explain that the use of the future tense indicates that the king's order that all were required to bow down to Haman specifically exempted Mordechai. The verse states: AND ALL OF THE KING'S SERVANTS WHO WERE AT THE GATE OF THE KING'S PALACE WOULD KNEEL AND BOW TO HAMAN, FOR THE KING HAD SO ORDERED. AND MORDECHAI WOULD NOT KNEEL NOR BOW — i.e., Mordechai was not required to do so. Haman, however, never revealed this to Mordechai who was unaware of the fact that he was not required to kneel or bow. We see that when Haman told the king that the Jews were failing to abide by his decrees, he did not mention Mordechai's failure to comply with this specific decree. Rather, he sought other grounds to slander the Jews.

AND THEY DID NOT TOUCH THE SPOILS (*Esther* 9:15) — Why did the Jews refrain from taking spoils and why is this mentioned three times in the *Megillah*? All of those who were killed in the war were descendants of Amalek and Jews are prohibited from deriving any benefit from Amalek. The Torah, in telling us of the war with Midian, mentions three types of spoil: *shevi* [captives], *malkoach* [goods] and *shallal* [booty]. The *Megillah* thrice repeats the fact that the Jews did not touch the spoils, to emphasize that they avoided all three types.

THE JEWS AFFIRMED AND ACCEPTED (ibid. 9:27) — If they affirmed, then obviously they accepted. Why does the verse tell us that they accepted? Our Sages explained: They affirmed now what they had previously accepted — i.e., they now voluntarily reaffirmed the acceptance of the Torah which had been forcibly confirmed when given at Mt. Sinai.

The merit of obliterating Amalek always lead to an acceptance of the Torah. After Yehoshua battled with Amalek at Refidim, the giving of the Torah took place. And after Mordechai's war with Haman, the Torah was accepted again.

FEASTING AND REJOICING

🧂 It is a mitzvah to have a festive meal on Purim which should include meat and wine.

🧂 This festive meal should be partaken of during the day; if one ate this meal at night, he has not fulfilled the obligation. However, on the night of the fourteenth of Adar after the *Megillah* reading — or on the night of the fifteenth in the cities that celebrate Purim then — one should also rejoice and eat a more elaborate meal than usual. The table should be set and candles lit. One should wear holiday clothing when eating at night, and surely when partaking of the festive meal during the day.

✿ It is customary to schedule the festive meal for the afternoon of Purim. *Minchah* is recited in the early afternoon and the meal is extended into the night. Most of the meal, however, should be eaten during the day.

🧂 If Purim falls on a Friday, the meal should be eaten somewhat earlier in the afternoon and should be completed well before Shabbos so that one has an appetite for the Shabbos meal that evening. Some people have a tradition of eating the festive meal until the onset of Shabbos. They then place a Shabbos tablecloth on the table, recite *kiddush* and proceed with the meal.

The miracle of Purim is inextricably linked with wine. Vashti's downfall occurred at a feast of wine, and Esther took her place. Haman's downfall occurred at the feast of wine which Esther made. This feast of wine served to rectify the transgression of the Jews who had participated in the feast of wine made by Achashverosh. The Sages therefore ordained that one should drink wine until the point of intoxication on Purim. They said: One must drink on Purim until he cannot differentiate between "cursed is Haman" and "blessed is Mordechai". However, if one's health might be impaired by drinking wine, or if one fears that becoming intoxicated might lead him to act irresponsibly, or that it might lead him to neglect to recite the proper blessings and pray, he is not required to become inebriated. Rather, he should drink more than he usually does and when he falls asleep because of the effect of the wine, he will have fulfilled the obligation, for one who is asleep cannot differentiate between curses and blessings.

✿ It is customary to eat vegetables on Purim, in commemoration of the fact that Esther ate vegetables when she was in the king's palace so as not to partake of the food served there. The verse states: AND HE DIFFERENTIATED FOR HER AND FOR HER MAIDENS FOR GOOD (*Esther* 2:9) — i.e., he gave her food that was different and that was good for her. This was also true of Daniel, Chananyah, Mishael and Azaryah when they were in the royal household in Bavel — they also ate vegetables.

Although it is laudatory to eat an elaborate and festive meal on Purim, it is preferable for one to be more generous in giving gifts to the poor than in making an elaborate meal or exchanging gifts of food with friends. There is no greater joy or more praiseworthy action than making the hearts of the poor, the orphaned or the widowed happy. One who brings joy to their hearts is compared to the *Shechinah*, as the verse states: TO BRING SPIRIT TO THE OPPRESSED, TO BRING LIFE TO THE HEARTS OF

THE DOWNTRODDEN (*Yeshayahu* 57:15) (*Rambam, Hilchos Megillah* 2).

Why is the Purim feast held in the afternoon rather than in the morning as is the case with the Shabbos or holiday meals? We delay the meal until the afternoon since people are busy with the mitzvah of exchanging gifts of food in the morning.

The Gaon of Vilna found an allusion to this in the *Megillah*. The festive Purim meal commemorates the feast which Esther arranged for Achashverosh and Haman. She scheduled her feast on the third day of her fast — two hours before nightfall. Whereas all of Israel fasted for three full days (seventy-two hours), Esther ceased fasting on the third day so as to participate in the feast. Esther told Mordechai: I AND MY MAIDENS WILL ALSO FAST THUS (*Esther* 4:16). The Hebrew word for thus — *ken* — has a numerical value of seventy (*kaf* = twenty, *nun* = fifty); i.e., I and my maidens will fast for seventy [hours rather than the full seventy-two].

THE SIGNIFICANCE OF THE FESTIVE PURIM MEAL

The festive Purim meal has special significance, for it elevates the soul as well as providing pleasure for the body. The *Zohar* writes that on Purim one can accomplish the same spiritual elevation with bodily pleasure that one accomplishes on Yom Kippur by afflicting the body.

The people of Israel are holy — physically as well as spiritually. Thus, it is fitting that Israel's physical actions be imbued with holiness, and that they be performed so as to sanctify and serve as praise of God. Our Sages maintained that God's praise is greater when it comes from the physical realm rather than from the spiritual realm. However, as long as Amalek exists, they corrupt the purity of Israel's actions and pollute them by introducing an element of sin into them. When Amalek's powers are weakened and they are subjugated, then Israel's physical actions are immediately imbued with purity and they are performed for God's sake alone — from this God's praise results.

The joy associated with the mitzvah of this festive Purim meal is especially great, for it signifies that Israel has rectified the sin which they were culpable for during the time of Haman — participating in the feast of Achashverosh. Had this sin not been totally rectified, they would have been required to atone for it by subjecting themselves to affliction. The fact that they have been commanded to bring themselves physical pleasure serves as a sign that they no longer bear a remnant of guilt for this sin. Moreover, they have purified their bodies and their actions to the point where it now becomes incumbent upon them to bring themselves physical pleasure through eating and drinking.

It is proper to engage in some Torah study before beginning the festive Purim meal. This is alluded to in the Megillah, for the verse states: THE JEWS HAD LIGHT (*Esther* 8:16). The Sages explained: LIGHT — this refers to the Torah.

UNTIL HE CANNOT DIFFERENTIATE

The Rabbinic obligation to drink on Purim until one reaches the point where he can no longer differentiate between "cursed is Haman" and "blessed is Mordechai" bears examination, for we find no similar obligation elsewhere. Why would the Sages obligate us to drink until we reach the point where we are no longer in control of our mental faculties? The Sages of later generations have explained this requirement in the following manner.

Israel's salvation at the time of Mordechai and Esther was not temporary. Rather, it reflected an eternal change in Israel's destiny. In the *piyut* recited on Purim, we say: You were our salvation eternally, and our hope in every generation. Until the time of Mordechai and Esther, Israel's future was weighed on a scale of sin and repentance. It was feasible that they might, God forbid, reach the point where they would be subject to destruction were they to commit a major sin and not completely repent.

At that point in time, Israel was on the verge of total destruction, for they had committed a series of major sins. They had prostrated themselves to Nevuchadnezer's idol and they had participated in Achashverosh's feast — a celebration arranged by that wicked king to glorify Israel's destruction. He had desecrated the vessels taken from the *Beis ha-Mikdash* by using them, yet the Jews did not refrain from joining with him in his revelry. After the feast, they acted sinfully until they reached the point where they were subject to total destruction. Their judgement seemed to be sealed, God forbid. But they repented wholeheartedly and the mercy of heaven was awakened and a path of salvation was opened for them.

At this time, the Divine trait of mercy came to God and said: "Master of the Universe. Your children have sinned and a harsh decree has been issued against them. Then Mordechai and Esther aroused them to perfect repentance and the decree was revoked. But what will happen if they shall again sin and there will be no one righteous like Mordechai and Esther among them and Israel will not know how to expiate their sins? Is it possible that Israel, Your children, shall, God forbid, be destroyed at that time without mercy!"

Immediately, the path of salvation was broadened and the salvation became eternal and the hope of every generation. Even if Israel's sin should be exceedingly great and rise to the very heavens — their enemies shall be unable to destroy them. Israel's enemies shall perish but Israel shall never perish. Even in that generation; they were not saved through their repentance, but through the traits of mercy and compassion alone. And these gates of mercy and compassion — once opened — shall never be closed again.

Just as the salvation that Israel enjoyed then did not come about through their merit, but through mercy and compassion, so too do we — through the manner in which we celebrate — demonstrate that our salvation is also based solely on compassion and mercy rather than our own merit. We eat and drink until the point where we lose our ability to differentiate even between left and right, placing our faith entirely in God who protects us and guards us from every enemy and tormentor, from sin and iniquity, now and forever.

In seeking to attain a level of loss of mental awareness, why do we strive to achieve the level where we can no longer differentiate between things which are so diametrically opposed — Haman and Mordechai? It is as if we are saying: "Even if we can no longer differentiate between things whose differences should be abundantly clear, we still know that we shall not lack salvation, that our hopes are not fruitless and that our joy is not unbased, for in God alone do we place our trust. Whether sober or inebriated, we fear no evil for You are with us forever."

The Sages offered a number of other allegorical and mystical explanations for the mitzvah of drinking to the point of being unable to differentiate.

Anyone can differentiate between "cursed is Haman" and "blessed is Mordechai". A person, however, must learn to recognize the various intermediate stages that are between these two extremes so that he can determine which matters incline towards good and which incline towards evil. If one had drunk enough on Purim so that these intermediate stages are no longer clear, he is considered to be sufficiently intoxicated to have fulfilled the obligation.

Alternatively, there are two ways in which holiness finds expression in this world — either through the victory of the just or through the downfall of the wicked. Our Sages said: Just as God's praises are expressed by the righteous in paradise, so too are they expressed by the wicked in purgatory. However, God, as it were, prefers the praises offered by the righteous. When Israel acts meritoriously, the righteous are exalted and it is their praise that is expressed; all are happy and the joy is complete. But when Israel lacks merit, their salvation is realized through the downfall of the wicked who are excessively evil and descend to purgatory. The entire world trembles in fear of God, but there is no joy. Thus, the happiness of "blessed is Mordechai" — of Israel being saved through her own merits — is greater than "cursed is Haman" — the salvation that comes when the wicked have been destroyed.

Nevertheless, the Sages ruled that on Purim one is required to drink until he reaches the point where he can no longer differentiate between these two types of salvation. Why? Because the downfall of Haman is completely different from the downfall of other wicked people. The joy that results from his defeat is as complete as that which results from the victory of the righteous. Haman is a descendant of Amalek, of whom the verse states: AND IN THE DESTRUCTION OF THE WICKED THERE IS SONG (Mishlei 11:10). When Amalek is obliterated, it is as if there is a revelation of the Shechinah in the world and it is therefore fitting that we celebrate.

Thus, there is no difference between the joy associated with "cursed is Haman" and that associated with "blessed is Mordechai". So that man might not be distressed that he has merited salvation because of the excessive evil of the wicked rather than through his own merit, our Sages ordained that he drink and forget the difference between these two sources of salvation.

WHY WE WEAR DISGUISES ON PURIM

✿ It is customary on Purim to masquerade and dress as non-Jews so that we not be recognized. Jewish customs are Torah, and we would not follow a custom unless there were valid and good reasons for doing so.

One of the reasons offered for this custom is that we thus demonstrate that even though we sometimes sin and act like the other nations, this is no more than an outward manifestation. Inherently, we remain faithful to God. This was true of the Jews of that generation; their worship of Nevuchadnezer's idol was no more than a masquerade and they remained faithful to God in their hearts.

Our Sages taught us: R. Shimon bar Yochai's students asked him, "Why were the enemies of Israel [a Talmudic euphemism for the Jews] of that generation liable to destruction?"

He answered: "You tell me!"

"Because they derived enjoyment from the feast of that wicked man [Achashverosh]."

He then asked them: "If that is the reason, then only those in Shushan should have been liable, but not those who lived elsewhere."

They said to him: "You tell us!"

"Because they bowed down to the idol."

They asked him: "Is there arbitrary judgement in this matter [i.e., if they bowed down to the idol, why were they forgiven]?"

He answered: "They only did so for appearance's sake. And God only acted in this way [i.e., by allowing Haman to threaten them] for appearance's sake" (*Megillah* 12a).

A homiletical link to the Torah is offered by some as the basis for this custom. The verse states: AND I WILL SURELY HIDE MY FACE (*Devarim* 31:18). The Hebrew word for hide — *haster* — is phonetically related to Esther. The Sages used this verse to point to an allusion to Esther from the Torah, and it also serves to allude to our custom of hiding our faces on Purim — the day of Esther.

Israel and Amalek represent two diametric opposites in the history of the nations of the world. But as is often the case with extremes, they seem to share certain characteristics. Esav — Amalek's progenitor both in terms of family and in terms of character — was prone to disguise his true self. He dressed in fine clothing, acted piously and spoke glibly — all the while hiding his wickedness behind a mask of deceit and cunning. The Torah states: FOR HIS MOUTH WAS A TRAP (*Bereshis* 25:28) — i.e., his speech and intent were not one and the same.

One finds the diametrically opposing trait among the righteous of Israel. Thus, David *ha-Melech* seemed to be a sinner, whereas, in reality, he excelled in personal piety. Yaakov's righteousness was so well concealed that even his father Yitzchak failed to recognize his true character. It was only when Rivkah revealed Yaakov's inner traits that Yitzchak gave him the *berachos* of which only he was truly worthy.

AL HA-NISIM

Since the festive Purim meal is a Rabbinic requirement, the

obligation to recite the *al ha-nisim* prayer in the Grace after Meals on Purim is more stringent than the similar requirement on Chanukah.

✍ If one forgot to add *al ha-nisim* to the Grace on Chanukah, one is not required to repeat it since the meals on Chanukah are not obligatory. On Purim, however, there is a Rabbinic obligation to eat at least one meal. Hence, if one forgot *al ha-nisim*, he would be required to repeat the Grace after Meals. However, if one said *al ha-nisim* at one meal on Purim, one is not required to repeat it if one forgot to recite it in the Grace after subsequent meals. Some authorities maintain that there is no requirement to repeat the Grace if one forgot *al ha-nisim* since the essential part of the meal is the drinking of wine over which *al ha-nisim* is not recited.

✍ In any event, when one reaches *ha-rachaman* in the Grace after Meals, he should add the *al ha-nisim* prayer. Though one began his festive Purim meal during the day, and it extended into the night, one still recites *al ha-nisim* in the Grace, for our considerations are based on when the meal began. Among Sefardic communities, however, it is customary to only recite *al ha-nisim* by day. [Regarding the laws pertinent to the addition of *al ha-nisim* in *Shemoneh Esreh*, see the chapter on Chanukah in Volume I.]

GIFTS FOR THE POOR

✍ It is a positive Rabbinic precept to give two gifts to two poor people on Purim; one gift to each person. Even a poor person who himself subsists on charity is obligated in this requirement.

✍ This obligation can be fulfilled through any type of gift: money, food, drink or clothing. Optimally, the gift should be substantial. If the gift is money, the amount should be sufficient to enable the poor person to purchase bread weighing the equivalent of three eggs. At the very least, each gift must be worth at least a *perutah.*

🙠 The gifts should be given during the day of Purim rather than at night. It is proper to give them after the reading of the *Megillah.* One should not give these gifts from money which has been set aside for donating to charity. However, one may add a small amount to the money which was set aside and then give the larger amount to the poor so as to fulfill the obligation. Money which one has designated for giving to the poor on Purim may not be given to another charity.

🙠 The obligation of giving gifts to the poor on Purim does not free a person from his general obligation to give charity. Even poor people are required to give charity at least once a year — aside from their obligation to give gifts to the poor on Purim.

🙠 These gifts should be given early enough so that the poor person can benefit from them on Purim and for the festive Purim meal. However, the recepient may use these gifts in any way that he sees fit.

🙠 The gifts should not be given before Purim, lest the poor person use them beforehand, in which case the donor will not have fulfilled his obligation.

🙠 We do not attempt to determine whether the recepient is indeed poor — whoever stretches out his hand is to be given a gift.

🙠 If there are no poor people in his community, the gifts which he usually gives should be set aside until he has an opportunity to give them to the poor. The obligation to give gifts to the poor also pertains to women.

EXCHANGING GIFTS OF FOOD BETWEEN FRIENDS

🙠 It is obligatory to send a gift consisting of at least two items of food to another person. This obligation pertains to both men and women. This mitzvah should be fulfilled on the day of Purim.

🖎 To fulfill this obligation, one must give food which can be consumed without further preparation. One may thus send cooked meat or fish, pastries, fruits, candy, wine or other beverages. The obligation cannot be fulfilled by giving money. It is praiseworthy to send gifts to as many friends as possible. It is preferable, however, to be more generous in gifts to the poor than to friends.

🖎 Poor people are also obligated in this requirement. If one has nothing which he can give, he should exchange his own food with that of his friend and they will both thereby fulfill this mitzvah.

🖎 It is proper that the gifts should be substantial enough to convey a feeling of respect. Thus, one should be careful not to send something so inconsequential as might insult the recipient.

🖎 It is also proper that these gifts be delivered by a third party rather than by the donor personally. Although the general rule is that it is preferable to fulfill a mitzvah personally rather than through an agent, this obligation is different. The phrase *mishloach manos* used in the *Megillah* implies that this mitzvah is best performed through an agent. [*Mishloach* is literally translated as *the sending of.*] Nevertheless, if one delivered these gifts personally, he has fulfilled the obligation.

🖎 Mourners are not obligated in this mitzvah. However, some authorities maintain that they should send gifts, provided that they are not a source of joy.

LOVE AND UNITY — A SHIELD AGAINST AMALEK
The mitzvos of exchanging gifts of food between friends and

giving gifts to the poor on Purim serve to commemorate the sense of love and brotherhood between Jews — a sense which Mordechai and Esther fostered among all of Israel when they were threatened by imminent destruction. When there is inner unity among Jews, even the wrongdoers among them become righteous.

Amalek's strength is only manifested among those Jews who 'tail along' and whose link to the Torah and its mitzvos has weakened. Haman — the epitome of Amalek's evil — thought that he would be able to destroy Israel after he had weakened them by causing them to sin. Even those who had not fallen into his trap would have been culpable, for they had not protested when their brothers had stumbled. When a rift developed between the Jews who had sinned and those who had not, Esther told Mordechai: GO AND GATHER ALL OF THE JEWS (Esther 4:16). If unity were to again become the hallmark of the Jewish people, then Haman would be unable to subjugate even those who had stumbled. When he would have attacked one, all of Israel would have felt the pain.

Our Sages made this point in regard to Yaakov: His ingathering and the gathering of his children saved him from the hands of Esav (Bereshis Rabbah 84). Whenever Israel is threatened by Esav and Amalek, salvation can be found in their gathering together and strengthening the love and unity that binds them.

Just as the Jews were saved in the days of Haman by gathering together, so too are we obligated, in every generation, to strengthen our inner unity so that our enemies cannot achieve dominion over us. The holiday of Purim is especially suited for fostering this sense of Jewish unity. The mitzvos of exchanging gifts of food between friends and giving gifts to the poor — obligations which strengthen our sense of community — were therefore made obligatory on this day.

HUMILITY AND GRATITUDE

People send gifts to friends because they feel a sense of gratitude towards them. When the Jews wanted to express their gratitude and joy when they were saved from Haman's plot against them, they said to themselves: "Through whose merit were we saved?" Each of them realized that it was not their personal merit that had brought about the rescue and thought, "It must be because of my friend." Out of the gratitude which they therefore felt for each other, they sent gifts, as if to say, "I acknowledge the debt that I owe you — through your merit I was saved!"

It is fitting that every Jew should see himself as being responsible when things go wrong, and should give credit to others when things go well. In this manner, all Jews become worthy and the feeling of love between them is strengthened; a strength which will bring the ultimate salvation.

YOM KIPPUR — A DAY LIKE PURIM

The significance of Purim is so great, that Yom Kippur — the most solemn day of the year — is compared to it. [*Yom* — a day, *Kippurim* — like Purim.] On Yom Kippur, Jews ascend to a level whereby they transcend the constraints of nature by denying themselves physical satisfactions and thus achieve atonement for the sins of the body. On Purim, this same level of holiness is achieved through eating and drinking — even man's physical satisfactions become imbued with holiness.

When weighing the attainment of holiness achieved through denial and affliction against that achieved through engaging in pleasurable activities, the latter is superior, for it requires an infinitely greater measure of striving and effort. In this sense, then, Yom Kippur can be seen as being less than Purim — like Purim, but not as great.

The commentaries point to another element that these two days share, albeit in inverted order. The fast of Yom Kippur is preceded by a mitzvah to eat and drink. Purim begins with a fast which is followed by a mitzvah to eat and drink.

PURIM AND THE *MEGILLAH* WILL NEVER BE ABOLISHED

Our Sages taught: All of the holidays will be abolished, but the days of Purim will never be abolished (*Yalkut Shimoni to Mishlei 944*).

The Sages also taught: All of the books of the Prophets and the Writings are destined to be abolished when the *Mashiach* comes, except for *Megillas Esther*. It shall endure like the five books of the Torah and like the orally transmitted Torah. And though all memories of the tribulations will be abolished, the days of Purim will not be abolished, for the verse states: AND THESE DAYS OF PURIM WILL NOT PASS FROM AMONG THE JEWS AND THEIR MEMORY WILL NOT CEASE FROM THEIR DESCENDANTS (*Esther 9:28*).

In what way is Purim greater than all the other holidays?

The festivals and holidays of the Jewish year are all sanctified through Israel. In the days to come, when all days will be like Shabbos, what need will there be for holidays? It would be like using a torch in the middle of the day! What can this holiness add to a world that is already filled with the light of holiness?

The light of Purim differs from that provided by the other holidays. Its source is a revelation of the holiness from above, rather than from the actions of Israel in the natural world. This light of holiness will continue to shed its aura even in the Messianic age.

❖ ❖ ❖

In what way is *Megillas Esther* greater than the other prophetic writings which will be abolished?

All of the words of the Prophets were intended to strengthen the teachings of the Torah and provide support for its mitzvos and laws. In the world to come, *Mashiach* will come and he will establish the religion of truth on its proper foundations. The words of the Prophets will be fulfilled and Israel will engage in the study and practice of the Torah in the purity that marked man before he sinned and before the admonishments of the prophets.

The *Megillah*, however, differs from the other works of prophecy, for it marks not the end of a chapter, but the beginning of the obliteration of Amalek. This chapter will only come to an end at the time of the future redemption, when God will grant Israel respite from the enemies who surround her. Then Amalek's memory will be completely wiped out, and the manifestation of God's name and His throne will be complete. Then all will recount the mighty actions of God in obliterating the memory of Amalek — from the time of Mordechai and Esther through the end of days.

End of Adar

CHAPTER FOUR

THE PUBLIC NEED

God is considerate of those whom He created. He therefore did not require Israel to make their pilgrimages to Jerusalem during the rainy season. All three Pilgrimage Festivals — Pesach, Shavuos and Sukkos — occur between spring and late summer, when the days are beautiful and the nights pleasant for travellers. All winter long, people are engaged in their pursuits — one with his fields, another with his vineyards, another with his gardens. As the month of Nisan approaches, all of Israel rejoices and says: "Come, let us go to the house of God." From the beginning of Nisan, the people set out from every corner of the land to ascend to Jerusalem to offer the Paschal sacrifice, to be seen before the Divine presence and to fulfill the other obligations which they had to discharge in Jerusalem.

On the fifteenth of Adar, agents of the government would set forth to make repairs to the roads that had been damaged during the rainy season. The highways were fixed for the pilgrims who would soon be ascending to Jerusalem as well as for use by those who had committed unintentional murder and were fleeing to the cities of refuge. The cisterns along the sides of the highways were opened so that there would be adequate water supplies for the travellers and their livestock.

Since the Pesach pilgrimage was the first major gathering in Jerusalem after a half year recesss [from Sukkos until Pesach], it was also set as a time for other public activities as well. For example, it was an opportunity for those who were involved in litigation to bring their cases to the great *beis din* in Jerusalem.

Cases involving capital punishment [which could not be adjudicated by the local courts] or the administration of lashes for the transgression of certain mitzvos were also adjudicated then.

Other public activities, which were only possible in Jerusalem, were also scheduled. For example: The redemption of objects consecrated to the Temple treasury, the examination of the *sotah* [a wife suspected of infidelity], the preparation of the ashes of the *parah adumah* [for use by those who had become ritually impure through contact with a corpse], the ceremony of the *eglah arufah* [brought by the elders of a city when a person was found murdered in proximity to the town and the assailant was unknown], the boring of the right ear of a Jewish indentured servant who refused to go free after six years of servitude, and the purification rites of a *metzorah*.

All of these activities were intended to purify Israel of defilement and transgression so that they might ascend to be seen before God on Pesach.

The involvement in public works from the fifteenth of Adar — in preparation for the upcoming pilgrimage — was not limited to agents of the government. Anyone who was desirous of furthering the public good had ample opportunity to serve. There were many pious individuals who devoted themselves to public works during this period. The Sages praised these people and said of them: Whomsoever benefits the community is assured that he will not become a cause for sin.

The following incident is related in the Talmud (*Bava Kamma* 50a).

It once happened that the daughter of Nechunyah, the cistern digger [he was referred to as such because he used to prepare cisterns at the side of the road for use by the pilgrims], fell into a deep pit of water. The people went and informed R. Chanina ben Dosa. During the first hour [when it was possible for her

116

still to be alive], he said: "She is well." In the second hour [when it was still possible for her to be alive], he said: "She is well." In the third hour [when she should have died if she was still in the water], he said: "She has come up!"

The people asked her: "Who brought you up [out of the pit]?"

She answered: "A ram [the ram offered instead of Yitzchak] came led by an old man [Avraham]."

They asked [R. Chanina ben Dosa]: "Are you a prophet?"

He answered: "I am neither a prophet nor the son of a prophet! I said to myself, 'Is it possible that something for which this *tzaddik* [Nechunyah] has worked so hard [i.e., the wells which he dug for the benefit of the public] should bring harm to his descendant!'"

A similar incident is recorded in the Yerushalmi (Shekalim 5:1).

There was once a pious man who dug wells and cisterns for use by travellers. One day, his daughter was on the way to her wedding and was washed away in the river. All came to console him, but he refused to be consoled. R. Pinchas ben Yair came and wanted to console him, but he would not accept his consolation.

He [R. Pinchas] said to them [to the townspeople]: "You consider this man to be pious!" [I.e., his refusal to accept the judgement of Heaven would seem to indicate that he is not.]

They answered: "Rebbi, this is what has happened to him."

He then said: "Is it possible that one who brought honor to his Creator through water should be punished by his Creator through water!"

Immediately, a report began to spread through the city. "The daughter of this man has returned!"

Some say that she grabbed hold of a branch which miraculously appeared and she was thus saved. Others say that an angel appeared to her in the guise of R. Pinchas ben Yair and saved her.

THE TWENTIETH OF ADAR

In the days of Shimon ben Shetach and Choni *ha-Me'agel*, the twentieth of Adar was set as a day of celebration. The background for this celebration is recorded in *Megillas Ta'anis*. (See the variant reading in *Ta'anis* 19a.)

On the twentieth [of Adar] the people were thirsty for rain and it fell for them. The Land of Israel had suffered drought and famine for three years, and though they prayed, no rain had fallen. They went to Choni *ha-Me'agel* and said to him: "Pray that rains should fall."

He told them: "Go and bring in the ovens used for Pesach so that they not be ruined [by the rains that are about to fall]."

He prayed, but rains still did not fall. He then drew a circle and stood inside of it like the prophet Chavakuk and said: "Master of the Universe, Your children have turned to me, for I am considered to be a member of Your household. I swear in Your great name that I shall not move from here until You have mercy upon Your children."

Drops of rain began to fall. His disciples said to him: "Rebbi, this is not what we sought . We seek not to die of famine [i.e., we need sufficient rains rather than a few drops]. It seems to us that these rains have only come so as to absolve you of your vow!"

He said to them: "My children, you shall not die [of famine]." He then said [in prayer]: "Master of the Universe, this is not what I requested. I seek rains that will fill the cisterns, canals and wells."

Rains then began to fall as if from buckets. The Sages estimated that each drop was the size of a *log*!

They then told him: "This is not what we sought. We seek not to die. It seems to us that this rain has only come so as to destroy the world!"

He said to them: "My children, you shall not die." He then said [in prayer]: "Master of the Universe, this is not what I requested. I seek rains which bring bounty."

The rains then began to fall as usual. However, they continued to fall until the people of Jerusalem had to ascend to the Temple Mount [because of the flooding].

They said to him: "Just as you prayed for the rains to begin, pray that they should stop."

He answered them: "One cannot pray for good to stop. Rather, go and bring me an ox for a thanksgiving offering."

They went and brought him the ox. He placed his hands on the oxe's head and prayed: "Master of the Universe, look at Your people Israel, whom You removed from Egypt with Your great strength and mighty, outstretched arm. They cannot withstand Your anger nor Your abundant good. When You become angry with them, they cannot bear it. When You shower them with good, they cannot bear it. May it be Your will that there be relief."

Immediately, a wind began to blow and the clouds dispersed. The sun began to shine and the earth dried. The people went out into the fields and saw that the desert was covered with truffles and mushrooms.

Shimon ben Shetach sent him [Choni] a message. "Were you not Choni *ha-Me'agel*, I would excommunicate you! If these were years like those during the time of Eliyahu [when their was a Divine decree that there would be no rain], would God's name not have been desecrated through your actions! But what can I do? You plead before God like a son who pleads before his father who fulfills his wishes. If he [the son] says, 'Bring me warm food,' he [the father] brings it to him. If he says, 'Bring me cold food,' he brings it to him. 'Give me nuts,' he gives it to him. 'Give me pomegranates,' he gives it to him. 'Give me persimmon,' he gives it to him. Regarding you, the verse (Mishlei 23:25) states, LET YOUR FATHER AND MOTHER BE HAPPY, SHE WHO BORE YOU REJOICE."

PARASHAS PARAH

& The third of the four special Torah readings, *Parashas Parah* — the portion that tells of the laws of the red heifer — is read on the Shabbos immediately before the Shabbos on which *Parashas ha-Chodesh* is read. Thus, if *Rosh Chodesh* Nisan falls on Shabbos [in which case *ha-Chodesh* is read then], *Parashas Parah* is read on the last Shabbos in Adar. If *Rosh Chodesh* Nisan falls on a weekday [in which case *ha-Chodesh* is read on the last Shabbos of Adar], then *Parashas Parah* is read on the next to the last Shabbos in Adar.

& On the Shabbos that *Parashas Parah* is read, two Torah scrolls are taken from the *aron kodesh*. Seven people are called for the reading of the regular *sidrah* from the first scroll. The *maftir* then reads *Parashas Parah* (from the *sidrah* of *Chukas*) from the second scroll.

& There is a minority opinion that maintains that the reading of *Parashas Parah* is a Torah requirement. Hence, a minor should not be called as *maftir*. Since he is not obligated in mitzvos, he cannot discharge the obligations of those who are.

The reason we read *Parashas Parah* before Nisan is to remind those who have become ritually impure through contact with a corpse that they must purify themselves so that they might offer the Paschal sacrifice at the proper time.

The reading was established sufficiently before Pesach so that even those who lived far from Jerusalem [and left on the pilgrimage on *Rosh Chodesh* Nisan] would also be reminded that if they had become ritually impure, they would need to be purified through the ashes of the *parah adumah*.

Although the *Beis ha-Mikdash* has been destroyed and we no longer bring sacrifices nor ritually purify ourselves so as to be able to eat sanctified foods, we still study the laws and mitzvos of purification. By doing so, it is as if we have purified ourselves of our defilement and have prepared ourselves to offer our sacrifices.

The Yerushalmi relates: By right, *Parashas ha-Chodesh* should be read before *Parashas Parah*, for the Tabernacle was first put into use on the first of Nisan, whereas the *parah adumah* was first prepared on the second of Nisan. We read *Parashas Parah* first because its subject is the purification of Israel which enables them to bring the Paschal sacrifice at the proper time.

THE *PARAH ADUMAH*

The Torah only requires the use of the ashes of the *parah adumah* for one who became ritually impure through contact with a corpse. One who became ritually impure through other sources can become purified through the other means specified in the Torah.

This mitzvah was given to Israel on *Rosh Chodesh* Nisan in the second year after they had left Egypt — on the day when the Tabernacle was first put into use. At that time, all of Israel — including those who had not come into contact with a corpse — had to be ritually purified with the mixture of the ashes of the *parah adumah* and spring water, for they had all been defiled through the incident of the golden calf. Idolatry imparts the same type of ritual impurity as does contact with the dead.

When God became reconciled with Israel and commanded them to build the Tabernacle so that He might dwell in their midst, He gave them this mitzvah as a means of purifying themselves.

From the time when this mitzvah was first given until the destruction of the second *Beis ha-Mikdash*, there were nine red heifers. The first one was prepared by Moshe *Rabbenu* and its ashes were used for the entire period during which the first *Beis ha-Mikdash* stood. A small amount remained afterwards and was safeguarded as a remembrance.

The second *parah adumah* was prepared by Ezra the Scribe. The remaining seven were prepared in the years between Ezra and the destruction of the second *Beis ha-Mikdash*. The tenth *parah adumah* will be prepared by the *Mashiach*, may he come speedily in our days. Each time that the ashes of a *parah adumah* were prepared, some of the ashes from all of the preceding *paros adumos* were sprinkled on the *kohen* preparing it. This could only be done by a person who had never been ritually defiled through contact with a corpse. Similarly, the vessels used for the sprinkling were required to be made of stone which cannot become ritually impure.

Many of the mitzvos of the Torah are referred to as *chukim* — statutes — for they seem to have no apparent reason. Nevertheless, the reasons for them, as well as the mystical meanings that they convey, were revealed to the Sages, beginning with Moshe. As regards the *parah adumah*, however, the verse (*Bemidbar* 19:2) states: THIS IS THE STATUTE OF THE TORAH — i.e., this specific *chok* is different than all the others for its reason and meaning remain hidden.

The very essence of the *parah adumah* seems to point to a contradiction that is beyond our ability to resolve.

The Sages taught: All those who are involved in the preparation of the *parah adumah* — at every stage — become ritually impure, but the *parah adumah* itself renders people pure! [This would seem to be illogical, for if the *parah adumah* purifies, why would the people engaged in its preparation become impure?] God said, "I have established a statute, I have decreed a decree and you may not violate that which I have decreed!" (*Yalkut Shimoni* to *parashas Chukas* 759).

ALL THIS I SOUGHT TO ATTAIN THROUGH WISDOM. I THOUGHT I WOULD UNDERSTAND, BUT IT IS BEYOND ME (*Koheles* 7:23). Shelomo said: "I have reached the level of understanding all of the Torah, but this portion of *parah adumah* — as much as I strived, I expounded, I investigated and I asked — I THOUGHT I WOULD UNDERSTAND, BUT IT IS BEYOND ME (ibid.).

AND THEY SHALL TAKE UNTO YOU A PARAH ADUMAH (*Bemidbar* 19:2) — God said to Moshe: UNTO YOU I have revealed the reason, but for others, it is a statute (*Yalkut Shimoni* to *parashas Chukas* 759).

Come and see how Israel differs from the other nations of the world. Other nations praise a law when they understand its reason, and when they do not understand its reason, they hold it in disregard. In either case, they do not accept the obligation of the mitzvos upon themselves and do not observe them. They, and Satan, especially ridicule Israel regarding the mitzvah of *parah adumah*, saying: "What is this mitzvah and what is the reason for it?"

But Israel's character is different. They accept the yoke of the mitzvos whether they understand the reasons or not. A mitzvah whose reason is not specified is especially precious to them, for it is seen as being entirely a Divine decree.

The people of Israel belittle themselves in the face of Divine decrees and do not seek to understand the reasons for them, and they hold precious even those statutes which seem to contradict human reason. They adhere to them even if they do not see the wisdom of them and they follow God by virtue of their faith alone. Moreover, they fulfill even those mitzvos whose reasons they do understand solely because they are the will of God.

Israel is therefore worthy of the purity which descends upon them from heaven and which refines their bodies, their spirits and their souls. They become like a new creation which can transcend the natural constraints that limit others. Just as they nullify their own natures and reason in the face of God's will, so too does He rescind the constraints of nature on their behalf.

Although the meaning of the mitzvah of the *parah adumah* was revealed to Moshe alone, the Sages pointed to a number of allusions that can be seen from the regulations concerning its preparation.

Why are male animals used for most offerings, while this mitzvah is fulfilled with a female? R. Ivo explained: It can be compared to the son of a maidservant who dirtied the palace of the king. The king said [when he saw the dirt]: "Let the mother come and clean up the excrement!" Similarly, God said: "Let the heifer come and atone for the sin of the [golden] calf!" (ibid.).

The later commentators offered an alternative lesson that is alluded to in the laws of the *parah adumah*.

Through this mitzvah, the Torah teaches us the path of complete repentance that one must follow after having sinned. It demonstrates how one can erase the sin completely so that it leaves no impression whatsoever.

When man sins, his misdeeds leaves a mark on his soul —

even if he subsequently regrets what he has done. Moreover, one sin leads to another and his sin can cause others to sin as well. They, in turn, lead others to sin. Thus, a single sin can cause the entire creation to become deficient. How then can man remove his own sin from the world and erase all traces of its effects?

The path of *teshuvah* — repentance — is as follows: Man must first forsake his own sin and not repeat it. He must then examine what it was that caused him to sin and rectify that. To whatever extent possible, he must trace the causes as far back as he can. If he reaches the original cause and rectifies that, he will have achieved purity and will erase the deficiency which he has brought into the world.

This process is alluded to by the procedure in which the *parah adumah* was prepared. Israel had committed the sin of worshipping the golden calf. After having repented, they burned it in fire and nullified it. They then began to go back to its source — the red heifer [red being symbolic of sin]. They burned this heifer until it became ashes but they still had not reached the original cause. They therefore placed the ashes into spring water and poured the mixture into a consecrated vessel. They had thus reached the root of all creation — the "living" waters of creation, as the verse (*Bereshis* 1:2) states: AND THE SPIRIT OF GOD HOVERS UPON THE SURFACE OF THE WATERS. Having reached this root, all becomes pure and all is rectified.

Thus, a man who has sinned must free himself of the sin and all of its causes and must consider himself as a new being. It is as if he had just been born into a world that had just been created. The only thing that preceded him is the root, the "living" waters free of earth or ashes or any of their derivations, which were placed into the sanctified vessel fashioned for them by the Creator alone.

THE DAYS OF DEDICATION

The last seven days of Adar — from the twenty-third until *Rosh Chodesh* Nisan — are called the "days of dedication". It was then that Moshe *Rabbenu* consecrated the Tabernacle after its construction. On *Rosh Chodesh* Nisan, the Tabernacle began to be used and Aharon and his sons began to serve as *kohanim*. During the seven days of dedication, Moshe served as the *kohen*. He would build it and then take it apart, offer the sacrifices of consecration, eat the sanctified portions and perform all of the service of the *kohen gadol*.

These days of dedication of the first Tabernacle of God — constructed by Moshe at God's command — are destined to be repeated when the *Mashiach* comes. His coming and the building of the *Beis ha-Mikdash* will take place in the month of Nisan. Thus, the days of dedication serve as a memorial to the Tabernacle made by Moshe as well as a time of prayer for the final redemption and the rebuilding of the *Beis ha-Mikdash* in which His *Shechinah* shall reside forever.

THE TWENTY-EIGHTH OF ADAR

The twenty-eighth of Adar is recorded as the day on which the Jews were informed of the annulment of a number of harsh decrees in the times of the Roman occupation of the Land of Israel.

It once happened that a series of decrees was issued prohibiting the study of Torah, the circumcision of children and the observance of Shabbos. What did Yehudah ben Shamua and his colleagues do? They sought advice from a wealthy woman who was friendly with all of the important people in Rome.

She told them: "Go out at night [when the Romans are celebrating] and shout in supplication."

They went out at night and shouted: "By heaven, are we not brothers? Are we not descended from the same father? Why are we different than every other nation that you oppress us with such harsh decrees?"

The decrees were annulled and the day was established as a festival (Ta'anis 18a).

ADAR II

🪶 All of the laws applicable to Adar apply to Adar II in a leap year. Thus, Purim and the four special Torah readings take place in Adar II. Those who have a custom of fasting on the seventh of Adar in commemoration of the death of Moshe, do so on the seventh of Adar II. In *Yalkut Yehoshua*, however, a tradition is cited that Moshe died on the seventh of *Adar* I in a leap year. Thus, in leap years, the anniversary of his death would fall on the seventh of Adar I.

✿ Although, as we have noted, Purim is celebrated in Adar II, it is customary to observe the fourteenth and fifteenth of Adar I with some festive spirit. Hence, we do not say *tachanun* on these days, nor do we fast or permit eulogies.

🪶 If one was born in the month of Adar during a regular year, and he turns thirteen in a leap year, he does not become bar mitzvah until Adar II. However, if he was born in a leap year, his bar mitzvah is in the month of his birth. It is therefore possible — in the case of children born but a day apart — that the bar mitzvah of the younger child will take place almost an entire month before the bar mitzvah of the older child! Similarly, it is possible — in the case of children born almost a month apart — that the bar mitzvah of the younger child will precede the bar mitzvah of the older child.

For example, let's say that two children were born in a leap year — one on the last day of Adar I and the second on *Rosh*

Chodesh Adar II, and they turn thirteen in a regular year. The bar mitzvah of the younger child will take place on *Rosh Chodesh* Adar, whereas the bar mitzvah of the older child will take place on the last day of Adar! Or, let's say that the children were born in a leap year — one on the twenty-eighth of Adar I and the second one on the twenty-seventh of Adar II, almost a month later. If they become thirteen in a regular year, the bar mitzvah of the younger child will be a day before that of the older child!

❖ ❖ ❖

Why is Purim celebrated in Adar II in leap years rather than in Adar I? Some explain that Haman's decree was issued in a leap year during Adar II. Others explain that we observe Purim during Adar II so as to celebrate the redemption of Esther in proximity to the redemption from Egypt.

❖ ❖ ❖

Why do we create a leap year by adding an extra Adar rather than some other month? As we have explained [see the chapter on *Rosh Chodesh*], the purpose of establishing leap years is to insure that the month of Nisan should always fall in the spring, for the Torah — in commanding us to celebrate Pesach — states: OBSERVE THE [FESTIVAL OF THE] MONTH OF SPRING (*Devarim* 16:1).

Were we to add an extra month to Shevat or Teves, for example, and spring were to arrive in Adar, the *beis din* might have cause to regret having established the leap year. By Adar, however, we can tell whether the winter is over — and a leap year need not be declared — or whether it will be prolonged — in which case an extra month is added to insure that Nisan falls in spring.

Although our calendar today is based on calculation rather than on seasonal observation, we do not depart from the principles that the *Sanhedrin* followed in setting the calendar.